Guitar Theory
WORKBOOK

An Easy Guide to the Basics of Music Theory for All Guitarists

by
Burgess Speed

To access audio visit:
www.halleonard.com/mylibrary
Enter Code
"3980-4958-3458-1237"

ISBN 978-1-4950-6281-0

Visit Hal Leonard Online at
www.halleonard.com

Contact us:
Hal Leonard
7777 West Bluemound Road
Milwaukee, WI 53213
Email: info@halleonard.com

In Europe, contact:
Hal Leonard Europe Limited
42 Wigmore Street
Marylebone, London, W1U 2RN
Email: info@halleonardeurope.com

In Australia, contact:
Hal Leonard Australia Pty. Ltd.
4 Lentara Court
Cheltenham, Victoria, 3192 Australia
Email: info@halleonard.com.au

CONTENTS

INTRODUCTION

Welcome to the *Guitar Theory Workbook*, a simple beginner's guide to music theory for guitarists. Everything in this book is geared toward the guitar so that you're able to apply the theoretical concepts directly to your instrument. A little knowledge of the guitar is helpful, but we have covered the basics so that, even if you are just starting guitar, the *Guitar Theory Workbook* will be an invaluable companion to your regular lessons.

Music theory is fun. There is nothing better than to hear a song on the radio or somewhere else and understand its components, how it's made, and why it sounds good. Music theory is communicated, in part, via written music, so we will cover the basics in this book. In addition, we will look at:

- The way notes interact with each other
- How collections of notes form scales and keys
- How chords are created and how they function within keys
- How to identify notes, scales, and chords by ear
- The relationships of notes, scales, and chords on the guitar fretboard

We will look at many other concepts, as well.

COMPONENTS

Instruction

Every idea in this book is covered and taught in the easiest, most straightforward way. Wherever possible, the concepts are applied to guitar through the use of guitar-specific devices like fretboard diagrams and tablature (tab).

Assignments

There is nothing worse than having a ton of information thrown at you and being expected to understand and remember it. In our book, you apply each new concept through short assignments and quizzes so that as soon as a new idea is introduced, it is reinforced through application and practice. This helps to build a solid foundation and understanding.

Ear Training

Being able to identify and understand what you hear opens up a whole new world of possibilities for a musician. Before there were online guitar tabs, most guitarists figured out their favorite songs and solos by ear. Their love of music and their desire to sound like their musical heroes drove them to develop their musical ear, which is a muscle that requires exercise, practice, and consistency. The tabs you find online are often incorrect, so it is worth taking the time to develop the necessary skills for writing your *own* tabs.

Included in the ear-training sections are listening sections and ear-training quizzes, where you are asked to identify pitches, chords, and scales. You will even write down, or *transcribe*, simple phrases and melodies.

Answers

The answers to every question and quiz are included in the answer key. Take your time when answering all the questions, making every attempt to answer them yourself before checking the key.

Audio

The audio files provide examples for you to hear so you can associate the real sounds with the concepts. This is where you will hear all of the ear-training examples and quizzes. To access the audio files for download or streaming, simply visit **www.halleonard.com/mylibary** and enter the code found on page 1 of this book. The examples with accompanying audio tracks are marked with audio icons throughout the book.

Take your time when working through this book, giving each idea and section time to sink in. Use this book as a supplement to your other guitar studies. You will see how this knowledge illuminates all your other areas of focus.

Chapter 1: GUITAR BASICS

PARTS OF THE GUITAR

Since this book is about music theory as it relates to the guitar, we'll need to refer to the various parts of the instrument. Below are photos of an acoustic guitar and an electric guitar with their various components labeled.

Acoustic Guitar

Electric Guitar

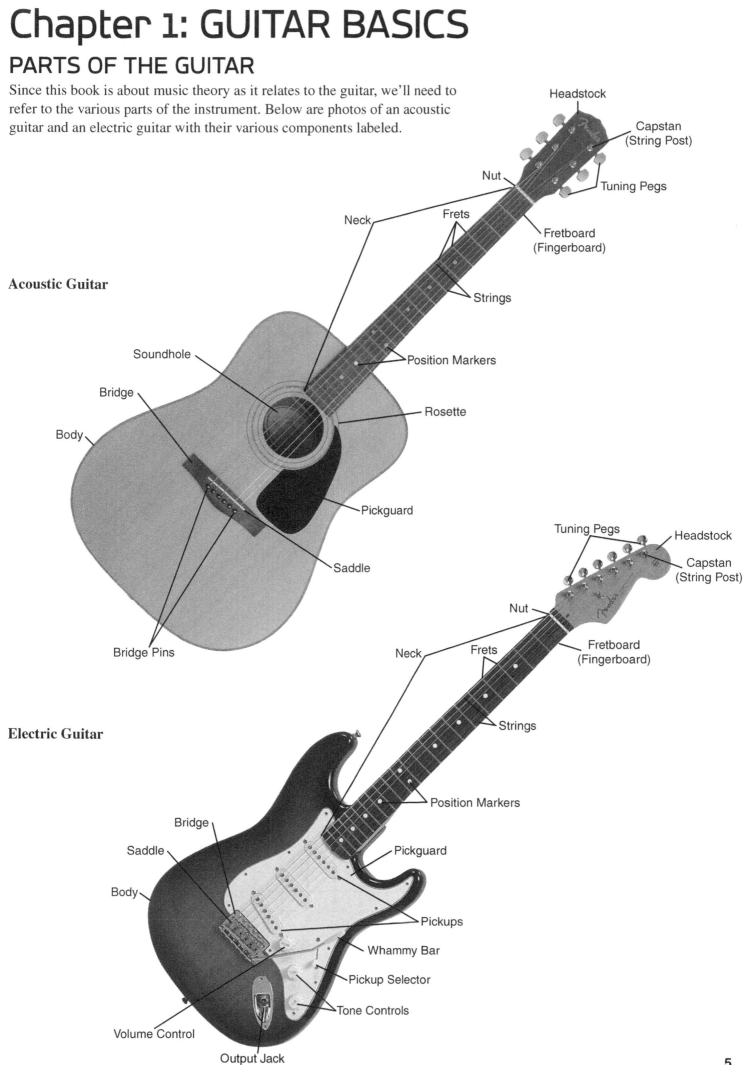

THE BASICS OF THE FRETBOARD AND FRETBOARD DIAGRAMS

The guitar fretboard lies on the neck of the guitar and is a cross-section of strings and frets. In fact, each time you press a particular string at a particular fret, it is like the intersection of an "x" and "y" coordinate on a map, which gives you an exact location. Fretboard diagrams, like the ones seen here, are sometimes used to convey musical "coordinates" on the guitar.

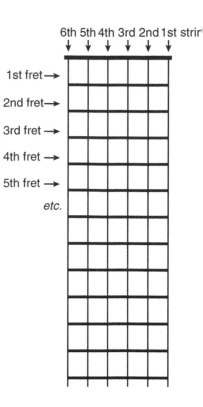

Strings

The vertical (up and down) diagram depicts a fretboard as if you were holding a guitar vertically, with the fretboard facing you. As you can see, there are six strings—represented by six vertical lines—with the 1st string being all the way to the right. The 1st string, which is also the thinnest, is the closest to the floor when the guitar is held horizontally (in playing position). The 6th string is the thickest and is closest to the ceiling when held in playing position.

Frets

In the diagram to the right, frets (which are divided on your actual fretboard with metal "fret wires") run horizontally across the fretboard, with the 1st fret being all the way at the top, the 2nd fret being under that, then the 3rd, the 4th, etc. When the guitar is held in playing position, the frets run vertically and the 1st fret is farthest away from your body.

The number of frets on any one guitar varies. Generally speaking though, acoustic guitars can have around 19 frets and electric guitars can have anywhere from 21 to 27 frets.

More About Diagrams and the Fretboard

You may also encounter fretboard diagrams oriented horizontally, like below. (For now, there is no need to know the specific applications for horizontal and vertical diagrams—we'll look at those later.) Here, the 1st string is on top; though, counter-intuitively, in playing position, this string is closest to the floor. (Yes, there are contradictions and information that is sometimes confusing when learning an instrument and music theory, but don't let it frustrate you—sometimes you just have to roll with it!) When a diagram is oriented horizontally, the 1st fret is always positioned to the left, and this is something that doesn't change.

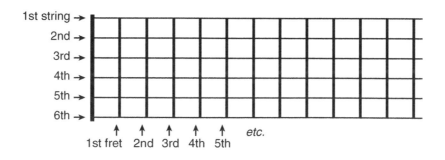

Additionally, sometimes you will see diagrams that start at frets other than the 1st. Below are a couple of examples, one starting at the 3rd fret, and the other starting at the 7th fret.

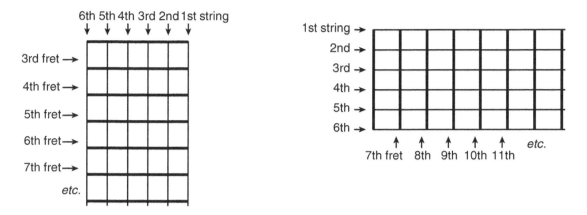

We mentioned earlier how diagrams are used to give musical "coordinates" on the guitar; that is, where (i.e., on which fret) to press a particular string. Dots, or more precisely, solid-black circles are used to indicate these coordinates. Check out the diagram below. If we read this from left to right (6th string to 1st), we are pressing the 5th string at the 3rd fret, the 3rd string at the 5th fret, and the 1st string at the 2nd fret.

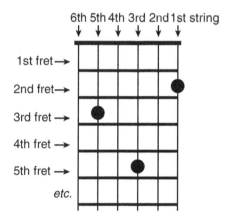

Let's look at another one. Below, if we read the diagram from the bottom to the top (6th string to 1st), we are playing the 6th string at the 8th fret, the 5th string at the 8th fret, the 4th string at the 10th fret, and the 3rd string at the 10th fret.

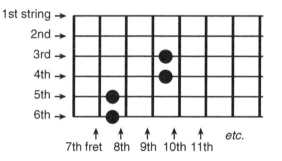

Typically, diagrams appear without all the strings and frets labeled—usually, there will be only a few (or one) fret indicators. Below is another example showing how a diagram might look. Here, you will be playing the 3rd string at the 8th fret and the 2nd string at the 11th fret.

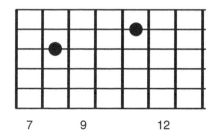

Assignment 1.1

Match the letters in the diagram with the acoustic guitar parts listed to the left.
Write the letter next to the appropriate part.

_____ Rosette

_____ Neck

_____ Soundhole

_____ Headstock

_____ Position Markers

_____ Tuning Pegs

_____ Bridge Pins

_____ Capstan (String Post)

_____ Nut

_____ Frets

_____ Saddle

_____ Body

_____ Bridge

_____ Pickguard

_____ Strings

_____ Fretboard (Fingerboard)

Assignment 1.2

Match the letters in the diagram with the electric guitar parts listed to the left.
Write the letter next to the appropriate part.

_____ Whammy Bar

_____ Neck

_____ Output Jack

_____ Headstock

_____ Position Markers

_____ Tuning Pegs

_____ Pickups

_____ Capstan (String Post)

_____ Volume and Tone Controls

_____ Pickup Selector

_____ Nut

_____ Frets

_____ Saddles

_____ Body

_____ Bridge

_____ Pickguard

_____ Strings

_____ Fretboard (Fingerboard)

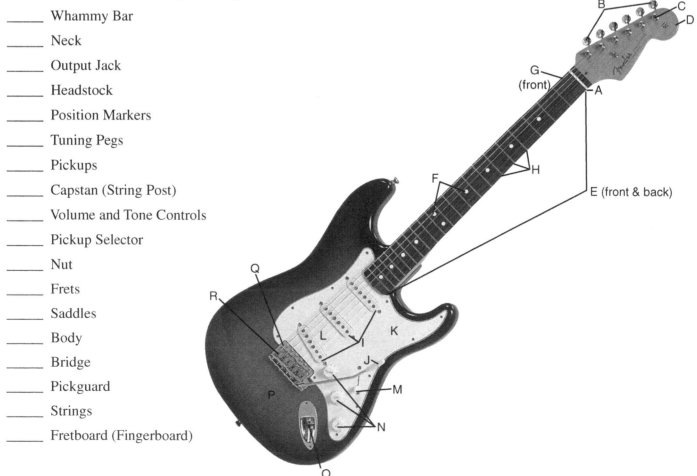

Assignment 1.3

The following diagrams indicate musical coordinates on the fretboard. On the lines to the right of each diagram, fill in the exact location of each coordinate. Read the diagrams from the 6th string to the 1st string. The first answer has been given.

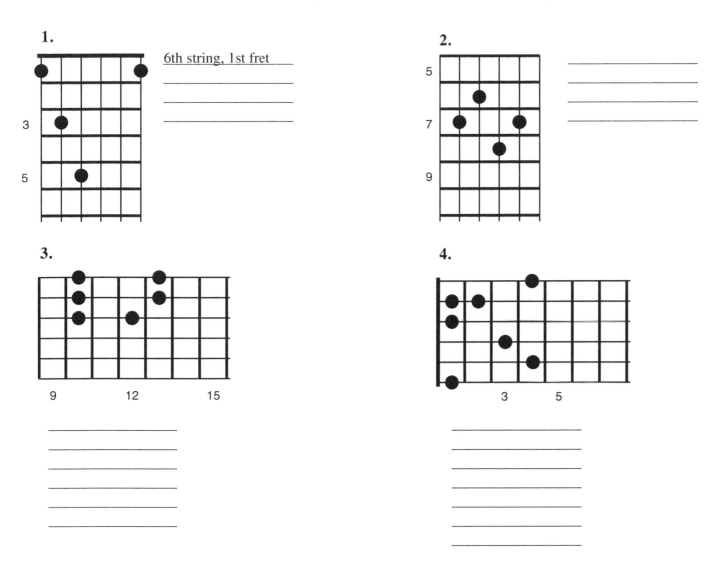

1.

6th string, 1st fret
_____
_____
_____

2.

_____
_____
_____
_____

3.

_____
_____
_____
_____
_____
_____

4.

_____
_____
_____
_____
_____
_____
_____

READING TABLATURE (TAB)

Another way to convey musical coordinates on the fretboard is *tablature*, also known as *tab*. While similar to fretboard diagrams in that it shows exactly which strings to play and at which frets, tab is different in that it can represent an actual piece of music, not just static information on a fretboard.

The tab *staff* consists of six horizontal lines, each representing a guitar string. The highest line is the 1st string and the lowest line is the 6th string. Numbers on the lines indicate which frets to press and on which strings. Check out the following example. Look at the numbers on the tab staff, along with the musical coordinates underneath.

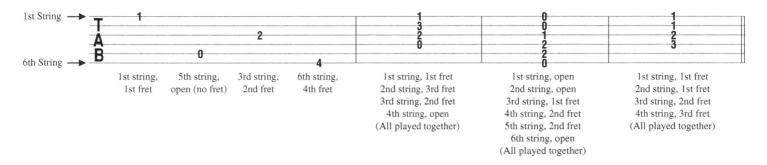

Although tab doesn't provide all the necessary information for a piece of music, it is a quick way to show guitarists exactly where to play the notes on the fretboard. In this book, we will include tab when appropriate.

Assignment 1.4

In the following two examples, look at the numbers on the tab staff. On the lines below the staff, provide the indicated fretboard locations. The first answer is given.

1.

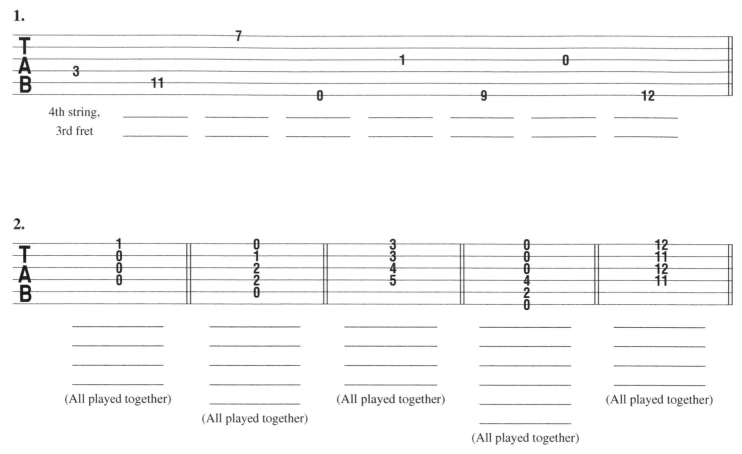

4th string,
3rd fret

2.

In Example 3, the fretboard locations are provided underneath the staff. Write these locations on the staff itself.

3.

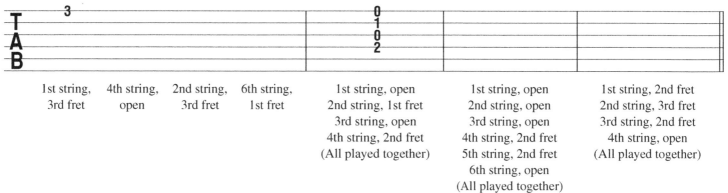

| 1st string, 3rd fret | 4th string, open | 2nd string, 3rd fret | 6th string, 1st fret | 1st string, open 2nd string, 1st fret 3rd string, open 4th string, 2nd fret (All played together) | 1st string, open 2nd string, open 3rd string, open 4th string, 2nd fret 5th string, 2nd fret 6th string, open (All played together) | 1st string, 2nd fret 2nd string, 3rd fret 3rd string, 2nd fret 4th string, open (All played together) |

Chapter 2: READING MUSIC—PITCH

In this chapter, we'll learn about the most universal method of reading and writing music: *standard notation*. Whereas tab indicates the exact location of a sound to be played on the guitar, standard notation leaves it to personal preference, because there are often several places on the fretboard where you can play the same sound—but more about that later!

MUSIC ALPHABET

The *music alphabet* consists of seven note names: A–B–C–D–E–F–G. (Shortly, we'll discuss actual pitches, but for now, all you need to know are the letters.) After G, the alphabet goes back to A and repeats. As you progress through the music alphabet, the *pitch*—the highness or lowness of a musical tone, or sound—ascends, or gets higher. To the right are a couple of examples of how the music alphabet progresses as it rises in pitch. The first example starts on the note A, and the second example starts on F. You can begin and end on any note of the music alphabet.

Of course, the music alphabet can go backwards, as well, in which case, the pitches descend, or get lower. For example:

ABCDEFGABCDE *etc.*

FGABCDEFGABC *etc.*

GFEDCBAGFEDC *etc.*

Assignment 2.1

In the following examples, fill in the blanks with the missing letters of the music alphabet.

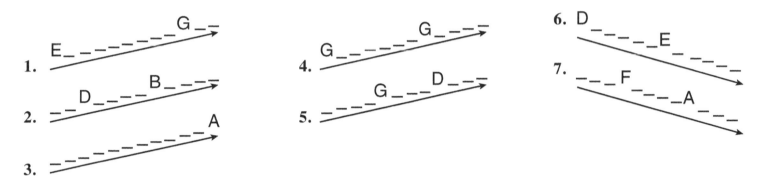

1. E _ _ _ _ _ G _ _
2. D _ _ _ _ B _ _ _ A
3. _ _ _ _ _ _
4. G _ _ _ _ _ G _ _ _
5. _ _ _ G _ _ D _ _ _
6. D _ _ _ _ _ _ E _ _ _
7. _ _ _ _ F _ _ _ _ A _ _ _

THE STAFF, CLEF, AND NOTES

Staff

Music is written on a *staff*, which consists of five horizontal lines and the four spaces in between.

Clef

Guitar music is written in *treble clef* (see picture to the right), also known as *G clef*, and the clef sign appears at the beginning of every line of music. The position of the clef on the staff determines the names of the lines and spaces. The "curl," or "tail," of the treble clef encircles the line that will be "G," and the other lines and spaces are determined from that point. See below:

Treble clef

G line

Try drawing the treble clef a bunch of times on the staff below. Follow the steps indicated at the beginning of the staff.

Step 1   Step 2   Step 3   Step 4

Line and Space Names

As mentioned earlier, the tail of the treble clef encircles the line that will be G. The other lines and spaces are then assigned names from the music alphabet relative to that G, as seen below.

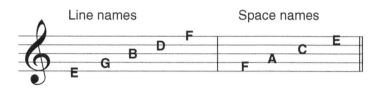

The line names can be remembered by starting the words of a phrase or sentence with each of the letters, for instance: **E**ven **G**ooey **B**ananas **D**eserve **F**udge. Of course, you can come up with your own phrase to help you remember. You try:

E_____ G_____ B_____ D_____ F_____.

FACE rhymes with "space," so the names of the spaces should be easy to remember.

As can be observed in the example above, the music alphabet progresses through the lines and spaces in this way: E (line), F (space), G (line), A (space), etc. So, once you know the name of any line or space, you can figure out the name of any *other* line or space by either ascending or descending through the music alphabet.

Ledger Lines

To indicate pitches that extend above or below the staff, ledger lines are used.

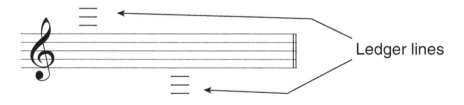

Ledger lines

The music alphabet progresses up and down the ledger lines and spaces, just like the staff.

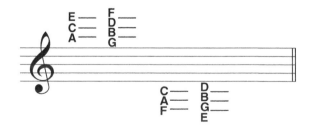

Notes

Pitches are indicated by writing *notes* on a staff. Notes appear in various ways and consist of different parts, including the *notehead*, *stem*, and *flag*. The appearance of these different parts determines how long the note will ring out for, but we will discuss that more in the next chapter.

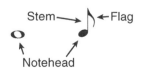

A note is named for the line or space on which it is placed. For example, if a note is placed on the B line, the note is "B," if it's placed on the E space, the note is "E," and if it's placed on the C ledger line, the note is "C."
Check out the example below:

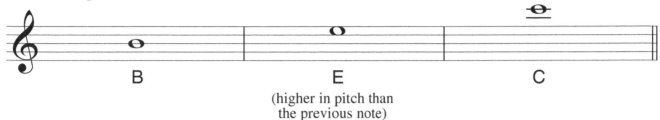

B   E   C

(higher in pitch than
the previous note)

As indicated in the example above, the higher a note's location on the staff, the higher its pitch (and the lower a note's location on the staff, the lower its pitch).

Assignment 2.2

Without looking at the original example, fill in the blanks with the correct names for the parts of a note.

Assignment 2.3

Fill in the blanks with the correct note names.

Assignment 2.4

Below each staff is a series of note names. Draw the corresponding notes in the correct locations on the staff. In some cases, like Example 1, there is more than one correct answer (both will be given in the answer key). Where ledger lines are present, you must use them to provide the correct notes.

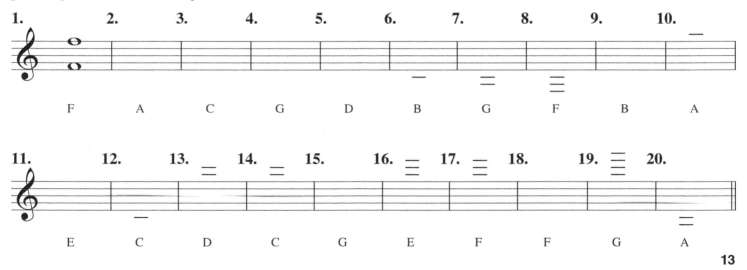

Assignment 2.5

Use the notes from Assignment 2.3 to answer the following questions.

Which of the following notes are higher in pitch:

a) Ex. 1 or Ex. 3 _____   e) Ex. 2 or Ex. 3 _____

b) Ex. 5 or Ex. 10 _____   f) Ex. 19 or Ex. 20 _____

c) Ex. 12 or Ex. 13 _____   g) Ex. 1 or Ex. 15 _____

d) Ex. 17 or Ex. 18 _____   h) Ex. 4 or Ex. 11 _____

Which of the following notes are lower in pitch:

i) Ex. 4 or Ex. 5 _____   m) Ex. 17 or Ex. 18 _____

j) Ex. 6 or Ex. 7 _____   n) Ex. 6 or Ex. 7 _____

k) Ex. 4 or Ex. 10 _____   o) Ex. 16 or Ex. 18 _____

l) Ex. 4 or Ex. 11 _____   p) Ex. 1 or Ex. 8 _____

Ear Training 2.1

Ear training is a process musicians use to develop their ability to identify, recognize, and understand the music they hear. Often, it takes the form of dictation, whereby musicians listen to music being played and then write what they heard. The highness and lowness of musical pitches, in relation to one another, is a perfect place to start your ear training.

 TRACK 1 (INTRO)

🔊 TRACK 2

Next to the appropriate example number, circle which note is *higher* in pitch, "Note 1" or "Note 2." If the pitches sound the same, circle "Same."

1. Note 1	Note 2	Same	6. Note 1	Note 2	Same
2. Note 1	Note 2	Same	7. Note 1	Note 2	Same
3. Note 1	Note 2	Same	8. Note 1	Note 2	Same
4. Note 1	Note 2	Same	9. Note 1	Note 2	Same
5. Note 1	Note 2	Same			

🔊 TRACK 3

Next to the appropriate example number, circle the note that is *lower* in pitch. If the pitches sound the same, circle "Same."

10. Note 1	Note 2	Same	15. Note 1	Note 2	Same
11. Note 1	Note 2	Same	16. Note 1	Note 2	Same
12. Note 1	Note 2	Same	17. Note 1	Note 2	Same
13. Note 1	Note 2	Same	18. Note 1	Note 2	Same
14. Note 1	Note 2	Same			

Fretboard Wisdom

When playing the guitar, if your fretting hand is moving toward the guitar's body, away from the headstock, you are ascending, or going up, the fretboard. If your fretting hand is moving away from the body, toward the headstock, you are descending, or going down, the fretboard.

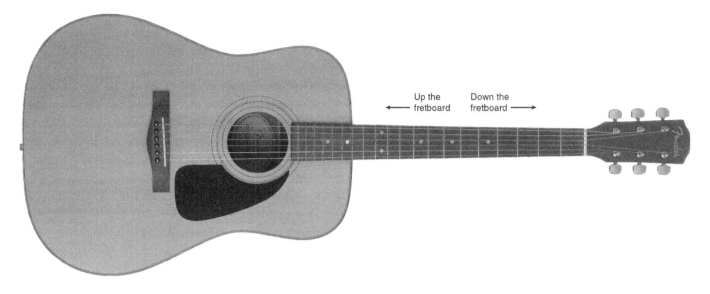

The fret numbers get higher as you go up the fretboard and lower as you go down the fretboard, as can be seen in the diagram below.

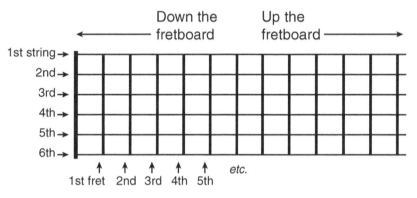

Exercise

1. On a single string, play a series of notes that go toward the body. In other words, play a series of notes that go up the fretboard. For example, on the 6th string, play a note on the 3rd fret, 7th fret, 9th fret, and 12th fret.

   What happens to the pitch as you go up the fretboard?

2. On a single string, play a series of notes that go toward the headstock. In other words, play a series of notes that go down the fretboard. For example, on the 6th string, play a note on the 12th fret, 9th fret, 7th fret, and 3rd fret.

   What happens to the pitch as you go down the fretboard?

Hopefully, you found that, on a single string, when you move up the fretboard, the pitch also goes up, or gets higher. When you move down the fretboard, the pitch goes down, or gets lower.

Chapter 3: READING MUSIC—TIME

Another essential aspect of reading music is time. Music exists in time, as pitches and silences all last for specific durations.

BEATS, MEASURES, AND BAR LINES

Music is felt in *beats*, which are like a pulse, or musical heartbeat. *Measures* divide music into small groups of beats (1, 2, 3, 4; 1, 2, 3, 4, etc.) and are demarcated by vertical lines called *bar lines*. *Double bar lines* indicate the end of a section or example, and *terminal bar lines* (or *final bar lines*) indicate the end of a composition. The organization of music in time is known as *rhythm*, and each measure can have a different rhythm, or combination of notes and/or *rests*.

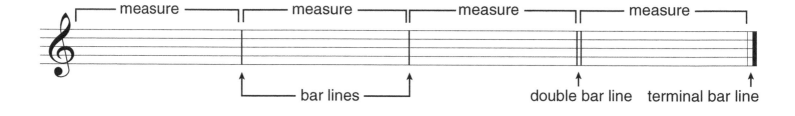

TIME SIGNATURES

A *time signature* appears at the beginning of a piece of music, after the clef, and indicates how the time should be counted. It consists of two numbers, one on top of the other, like a fraction. The top number indicates how many beats are in each measure, and the bottom number tells us what type of note equals one beat. Below are some examples of time signatures (we'll talk more about the different types of notes in the section that follows).

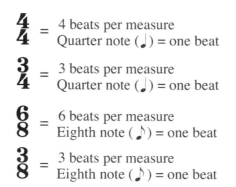

The most common time signature in Western music is 4/4. As a result, it is sometimes indicated by a "C" symbol.

NOTE VALUES AND REST VALUES IN 4/4 TIME

Let's look at the different types of notes and rests and their values in 4/4 time. The term *value* refers to the duration of the notes or rests—in other words, how long they last, or ring out. In the previous chapter, we covered the different parts of a note (notehead, stem, and flag). We mentioned that the appearance of a note determines its duration. Some notes will just be a hollow notehead, some will have a solid notehead with a stem, some will have a solid notehead with a stem and flag, some will have multiple flags, etc.

The following is a diagram showing the different types of notes and note values and how they relate to each other. Notice that, when eighth notes or sixteenth notes appear in groups of two or more, they can be *beamed* together. If there is one flag on the note (as with eighth notes), there will be a single beam; if there are two flags on the note (sixteenth notes), a double beam is used, etc.

Note Values

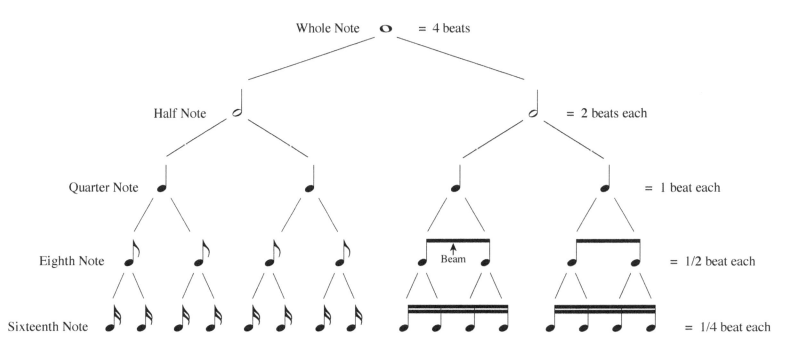

For every note, there is a corresponding rest, or silence. Below, you can see the different rests and rest values and how they relate to each other.

Rest Values

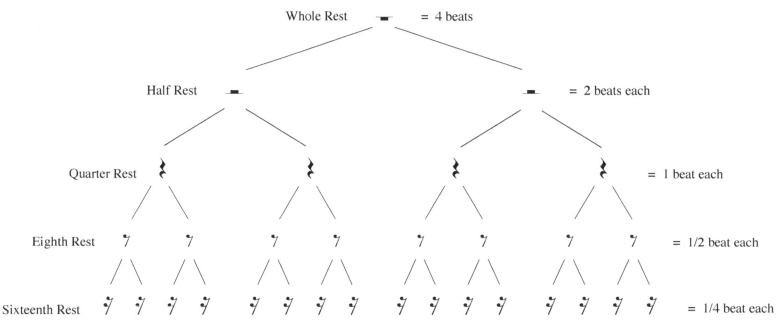

Counting Notes and Rests in Time

The following example demonstrates the correct way to count the various notes and rests in 4/4 time. The numbers are commonly called the *downbeats* and the ampersands (&) are commonly called the *upbeats*. (The formal definition of "downbeat" is the first beat of each measure, and the formal definition of "upbeat" is the last "&" in any given measure. However, we will use the common application of those terms and refer to the numbers as downbeats and the ampersands as upbeats.)

For the example below, try tapping your foot on the downbeats and simultaneously clap and count the various notes and rests.

 TRACK 4

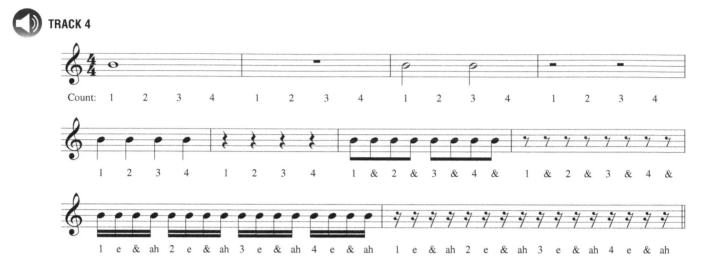

Triplets

A *triplet* is a group of three notes occupying the same time as two notes of the same value. So an eighth-note triplet is made up of three eighth notes that have the same time value as two eighth notes—in other words, one beat. An eighth-note triplet divides a beat into three equal parts that are counted "1 & ah, 2 & ah, 3 & ah, 4 & ah," etc. Triplets are beamed together and have a "3" above or below the group. When tapping your foot, be sure to bring the foot down on the downbeats.

 TRACK 5

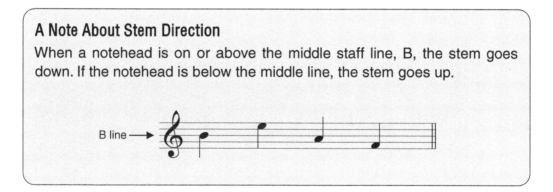

A Note About Stem Direction

When a notehead is on or above the middle staff line, B, the stem goes down. If the notehead is below the middle line, the stem goes up.

B line →

Notes and Rests in Music—For Real

There are many possibilities for how notes and rests can appear in a piece of music, and the ordering and arranging of these components is an essential part of songwriting and composition. The following is just one example of an arrangement of notes and rests and how they should be counted.

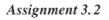 **TRACK 6**

Assignment 3.1

Look at the example below. Fill in the blanks with the appropriate terms from the provided list. Cross them out as you go to make sure you get them all.

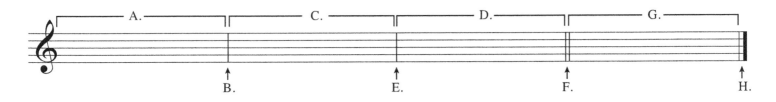

A. _____ bar line

B. _____ measure

C. _____ measure

D. _____ terminal bar line

E. _____ bar line

F. _____ measure

G. _____ double bar line

H. _____ measure

Assignment 3.2

Fill in the blanks with the correct word and/or number.

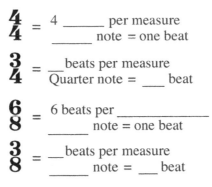

$\frac{4}{4}$ = 4 _____ per measure
_____ note = one beat

$\frac{3}{4}$ = __ beats per measure
Quarter note = ___ beat

$\frac{6}{8}$ = 6 beats per _____
_____ note = one beat

$\frac{3}{8}$ = __ beats per measure
_____ note = ___ beat

Assignment 3.3

Draw a line from each symbol below to its correct name.

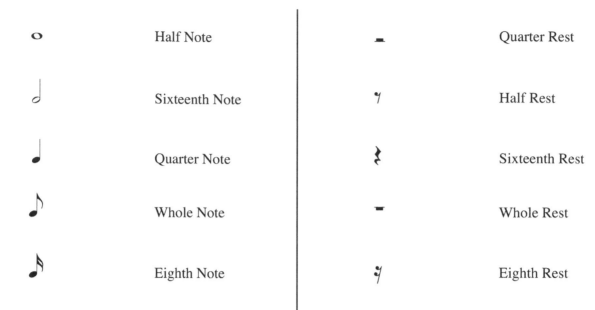

Assignment 3.4

Answer the following questions.

1. How many quarter notes can fit in a measure of 4/4 time? _____

2. How many whole notes can fit in a measure of 4/4 time?_____

3. How many sixteenth notes can fit in the space of a quarter note? _____

4. How many eighth notes can fit in the space of a half note? _____

5. Which lasts longer, a half note or a half rest? _____

6. How many eighth-note triplets can fit in the space of a half note? _____

7. How many sixteenth notes can fill a measure in 4/4 time? _____

Assignment 3.5

Fill in the blanks with the correct counting numbers and syllables; the first two are given.

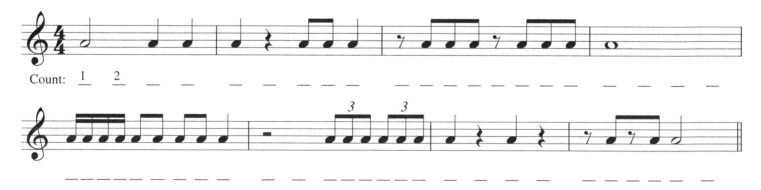

As another exercise, try clapping the rhythm above while tapping your foot on the downbeats and counting aloud. Listen to Track 7 to hear how this is supposed to sound.

 TRACK 7

Ear Training 3.1

For this ear-training session, you will *transcribe* what you hear in the accompanying audio. Musical transcription is the process of writing down, or notating, a piece of music that you hear. This takes practice, so don't get frustrated if it's not easy for you at first. The ear is a muscle, and ear training/transcription is the primary exercise for helping you to build that muscle.

When transcribing, listen to the examples and try to hum them back (or, for purely rhythmic exercises, clap them back). Listen to each track as many times as it takes until you have the entire exercise transcribed. When you think you have the exercise correct, listen along with the track and check your work. Make any corrections that you think are necessary before checking your transcription against the answer key.

For the following exercises, we are concerned only with rhythm. Use the A note on the second space for everything. The first two beats of the first two examples are given. Remember: stick with each example until you think you have it written down correctly.

TRACK 8

Ex. 1

TRACK 9

Ex. 2

TRACK 10

Ex. 3

TRACK 11

Ex. 4

TIES AND DOTS

A *tie* is a curved line connecting two notes of the same pitch, and it extends the value of the first note by the value of the second note (i.e., the two notes are added together). For example, a half note (two beats) tied to a quarter note (one beat) lasts for three beats; a quarter note (one beat) tied to an eighth note (1/2 beat) lasts for 1-1/2 beats; etc.

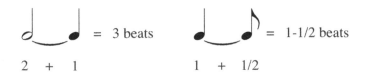

When a *dot* is placed to the right of a note or rest, it extends its duration by one half of its original value. For example, a dotted quarter note equals 1-1/2 beats (1 + 1/2 = 1-1/2). This can also be viewed as a quarter note tied to an eighth note (see below).

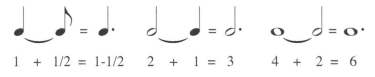

Here are some examples using rests:

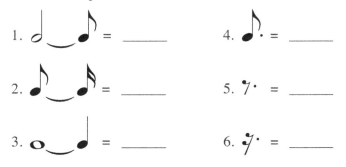

Assignment 3.6

Fill in the correct number of beats for the examples below.

1. ⬤ ⟶ ⬤ = _____   4. ⬤. = _____

2. ⬤ ⟶ ⬤ = _____   5. ⸰⸱ = _____

3. ⬤ ⟶ ⬤ = _____   6. ⸰⸱ = _____

Assignment 3.7

In the following examples, the bar lines are missing. Draw bar lines in the correct locations. Remember to check the time signature for the number of beats per measure.

Ex. 1

Ex. 2

Ex. 3

Ex. 4

Ex. 5

Ex. 6

Ear Training 3.2

Your next ear-training session features ties and dots, and you will be transcribing what you hear in Tracks 12–15. Notice that Examples 1 and 2 are in 3/4 time, which has three beats per measure. Remember to keep playing each track over and over until you have the whole example written down. When you think you have it all down correctly, check it against the track one more time and then against the answer key.

Again, for the following exercises, we are only concerned with rhythm, so use the A note on the second space for everything.

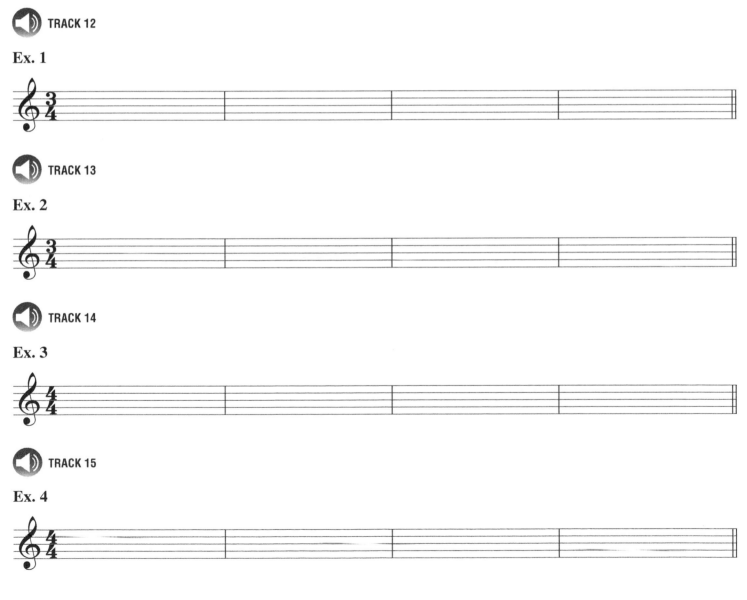

🔊 **TRACK 12**

Ex. 1

🔊 **TRACK 13**

Ex. 2

🔊 **TRACK 14**

Ex. 3

🔊 **TRACK 15**

Ex. 4

Chapter 4: HALF STEPS AND WHOLE STEPS

The distance in pitch between two notes is an interval. The two most basic intervals are the *half step* and *whole step*.

THE HALF STEP

On the fretboard, the distance between two adjacent frets—which is also the shortest distance between two notes—is a *half step*. Check out the diagram below:

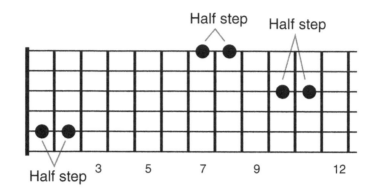

If you were going from the 7th fret to the 8th fret, you would be moving a half step *higher*. You could also say that you are going a half step *above* the note on the 7th fret.

If you were going from the 8th fret to the 7th fret, you would be moving a half step *lower*. You could also say that you are going a half step *below* the note on the 8th fret.

The diagram above uses only fretted notes to illustrate half steps, but there are half steps that include open strings, as well. When you go from any open string to the 1st fret (or vice versa), the distance is a half step. In the diagram below, open strings are represented with hollow (white) circles.

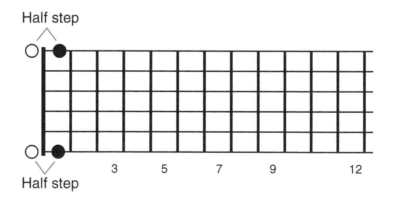

Assignment 4.1

In the diagram below, draw a circle one half step *above* each indicated note. (Remember: solid circles signify fretted notes and hollow circles signify open strings.)

Ex. 1

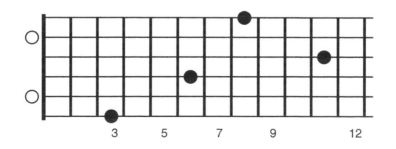

Now, draw a circle one half step below each indicated note.

Ex. 2

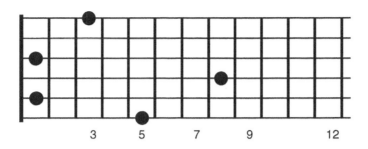

Ear Training 4.1

As mentioned earlier, the half step is the shortest distance between two notes, so it is very important for you to acquaint yourself with its sound. The half step is used in the famous theme from the movie *Jaws*. Check it out online if you haven't heard it before.

Listen to Track 16 to hear what the half step sounds like. You will hear examples moving to a note a half step higher and a half step lower.

 TRACK 16

Track 17 provides pitch pairs that are a half step apart. On the blank lines below, write whether the second pitch of each group is a half step *higher* than the first or a half step *lower* than the first.

 TRACK 17

1. _____   3. _____   5. _____   7. _____   9. _____

2. _____   4. _____   6. _____   8. _____   10. _____

THE WHOLE STEP

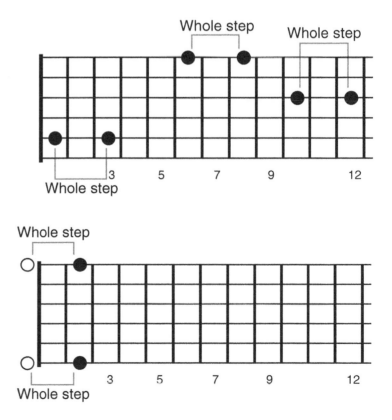

On the fretboard, the distance between two frets—with one fret in between—is a *whole step*. Typically, we refer to a half step as being a one-fret distance and a whole step as a two-fret distance. Check out the diagram on the right:

If you were going from the 6th fret to the 8th fret, you would be moving a whole step *higher*, or a whole step *above* the note on the 6th fret.

If you were going from the 8th fret to the 6th fret, you would be moving a whole step *lower*, or a whole step *below* the note on the 8th fret.

As with half steps, the whole-step distance can be between two fretted notes or an open string and a fretted note. When you go from any open string to the 2nd fret (or vice versa), the distance is a whole step.

Assignment 4.2

In the diagram below, draw a circle one whole step *above* each indicated note.

Ex. 1

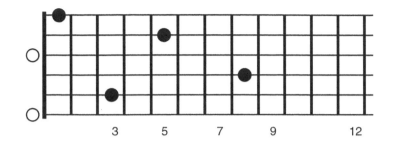

Now, draw a circle one whole step *below* each indicated note.

Ex. 2

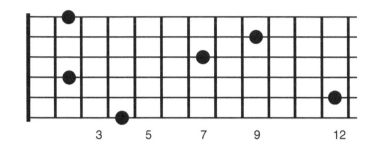

Ear Training 4.2

Like the half step, the whole step is an essential building block of music. In order to understand music when you hear it, you must recognize the sound of the whole step. The whole step can be heard in the opening riff of the Kinks' famous tune "You Really Got Me."

In Track 18, you will hear what the whole step sounds like, with examples moving to a note a whole step higher and a whole step lower.

 TRACK 18

Track 19 features pitch pairs that are a whole step apart. On the blank lines below, write whether the second pitch of each group is a whole step *higher* than the first or a whole step *lower* than the first.

 TRACK 19

1. _____   3. _____   5. _____   7. _____   9. _____

2. _____   4. _____   6. _____   8. _____   10. _____

DISTINGUISHING THE HALF STEP FROM THE WHOLE STEP

Now it becomes essential to know the difference, both visually and aurally, between the half step and whole step. This will help you immeasurably in your musical understanding and will provide crucial building blocks to recognizing more complex musical patterns later.

Visual Recognition

Check out the diagram below to see how half steps and whole steps look when placed side by side:

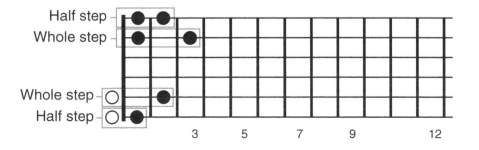

Assignment 4.3

Look at the diagram below. In the spaces beneath the diagram, write "H" for half step and "W" for whole step next to the corresponding numbers. For example, the space next to #1 corresponds to the two dots marked with that number in the diagram.

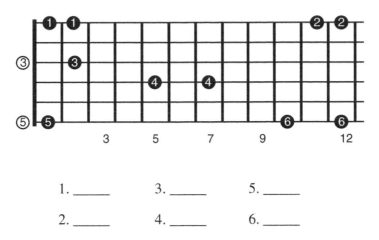

1. _____   3. _____   5. _____

2. _____   4. _____   6. _____

Aural Recognition

Ear Training 4.3

In this ear-training session, you will work on hearing the difference between the half step and whole step. Remember, as mentioned earlier, an example of how the half step sounds can be heard in the opening lines of the theme to the movie *Jaws* and the whole step can be heard in the opening lines of "You Really Got Me" by the Kinks. Check out those two examples online before proceeding.

To provide a solid basis for distinguishing between the half step and whole step, Track 20 features several examples of the two heard one after the other.

 TRACK 20

On Track 21, you will hear 16 pairs of pitches, all of which are either a half step or a whole step apart. Sometimes you will hear the lower of the two notes first, and sometimes you will hear the higher of the two notes first. If you are not sure whether a pair of notes is a whole or half step, hum the two notes and then see if you can fit a pitch in between them. If you cannot, then it is probably a half step. If you can fit a pitch in between, then it is most likely a whole step.

Pause the audio after each pair so you can hum it back and really let the sound sink in before deciding which step it is, whole or half. Write "H" for half step or "W" for whole step in the appropriate blank spaces below.

🔊 TRACK 21

1. _____   5. _____   9. _____   13. _____

2. _____   6. _____   10. _____   14. _____

3. _____   7. _____   11. _____   15. _____

4. _____   8. _____   12. _____   16. _____

Chapter 5: THE NATURAL NOTES

THE MUSIC ALPHABET REVISITED

The notes of the music alphabet (A–B–C–D–E–F–G) are the *natural notes*, which means they are not altered in any way. (In the next chapter, we will see what happens when you alter the natural notes.) On a piano keyboard, the natural notes are all the white keys.

Step Pattern for the Music Alphabet/Natural Notes

The distance between each of the natural notes is either a whole step or a half step, and this pattern of whole steps (W) and half steps (H) can be seen below.

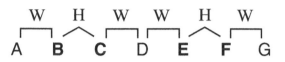

Note that the distances between B–C and E–F are half steps, and the distances between all the other notes are whole steps. Memorize this: **the distances between B–C and E–F are half steps**.

NATURAL NOTES ON THE GUITAR FRETBOARD

Names of the Strings

Let's begin to learn the locations of the natural notes on the fretboard by first looking at the names of the open strings and how they are written in standard notation. From the highest string (the one closet to the ceiling in tab) to the lowest, they are as follows:

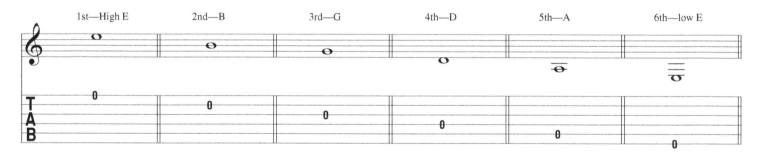

Here are the string names as they appear in a fretboard diagram:

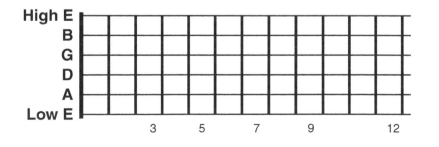

Step Pattern on Each String

As you've learned, you can start the music alphabet from any note. For instance, if we were going to start with the note E, which is the note produced by playing the open high-E string, we would get: E–F–G–A–B–C–D–E, etc. If we wanted to see where each of those natural notes lies on the fretboard, all we have to do is follow the aforementioned step pattern, starting with E. You could also put to work the memorized fact that the distance between E–F and B–C are half steps, and the distances between all the other natural notes are whole steps.

So, to find the locations of all the natural notes on the 1st string, you would follow these steps:

- **From E, go up a half step to F**
- From F, go up a whole step to G
- From G, go up a whole step to A
- From A, go up a whole step to B
- **From B, go up a half step to C**
- From C, go up a whole step to D
- From D, go up a whole step to E

Notice in the steps listed above, the half-step movements are in bold.

Below are the locations of the natural notes on the 1st (E) string:

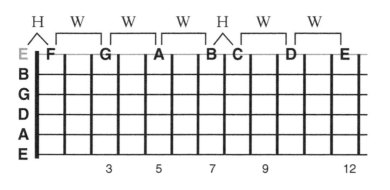

Now let's use the same approach on the B string:

- **From B, go up a half step to C**
- From C, go up a whole step to D
- From D, go up a whole step to E
- **From E, go up a half step to F**
- From F, go up a whole step to G
- From G, go up a whole step to A
- From A, go up a whole step to B

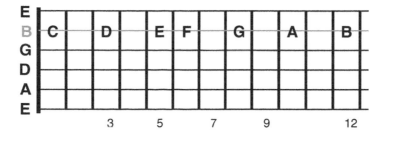

Assignment 5.1

Now it's your turn. The answers can be found in the complete diagram that follows, but avoid looking at it until you are done with this assignment.

1. Write the locations of all the natural notes on the G string.

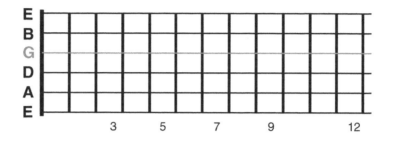

2. Write the locations of all the natural notes on the D string.

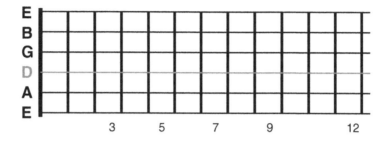

3. Write the locations of all the natural notes on the A string.

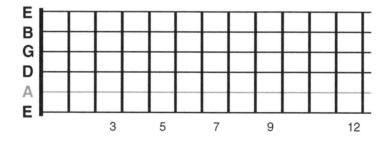

4. Write the locations of all the natural notes on the low E string.

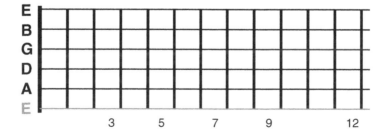

The Natural Notes on the Fretboard (Up to the 12th Fret)

Below is a complete diagram of all the natural notes on the fretboard up to the 12th fret. Using the approach covered on the previous page, you can figure out the rest of the notes *past* the 12th fret, all the way to the end of your fretboard.

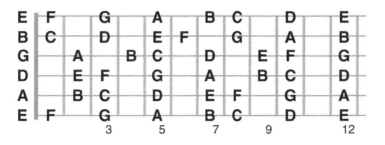

Another fact to memorize: **the locations of the notes on the 1st (high E) and 6th (low E) strings are exactly the same**.

So, if you know the note names on one string, you know them on the other, as well!

Ear Training 5.1

Simple Melody

OK, now that you have some practice recognizing rhythms, note/rest values, half steps, and whole steps, we are going to play some simple *melodies* for you to transcribe. A *melody* is a sequence of single notes, usually varying in pitch.

We will keep these melodies very simple at first and then build on them. We will give the first note of every example (the A note on the 2nd fret of the 3rd string), then you must use your knowledge of time signatures and note/rest values, as well as your ability to distinguish between half steps and whole steps, to figure out the remainder. Feel free to use your guitar to try to figure out the notes. Developing this ability will free you from the need to find online tabs to learn how to play something.

Listen to Track 22 and follow along with the music below. This will help prepare you for the exercises that follow.

TRACK 22

Like the example above, all of the following melodies will be *stepwise*, meaning they will move up or down the notes of the music alphabet—without any leaps or jumps. For instance, you will not jump from A to C or from D to G, etc. Also, remember when writing stems, if the notehead is below the B (middle) line, the stem points up; if the notehead is on or above the B line, the stem points downward. In the audio, a count of four (1, 2, 3, 4) will be given before each example in 4/4, and a count of three (1, 2, 3) will precede the example in 3/4 time.

TRACK 23

Ex. 1

TRACK 24

Ex. 2

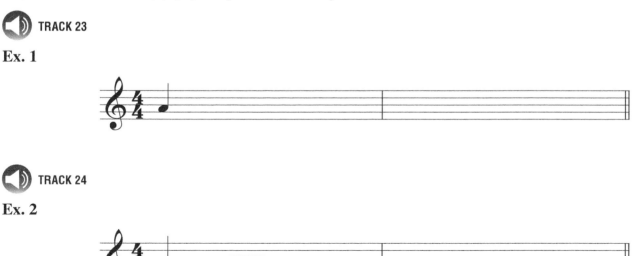

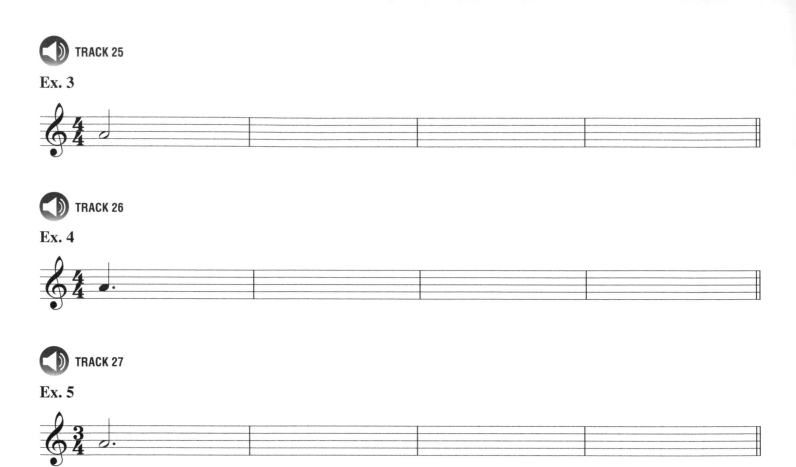

TRACK 25

Ex. 3

TRACK 26

Ex. 4

TRACK 27

Ex. 5

Chapter 6: IDENTICAL PITCHES AND NOTE NAMES

OCTAVES ON SINGLE STRINGS

Let's look again at all the natural notes on the fretboard:

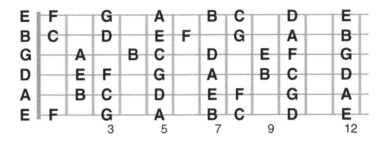

Notice that there are many locations with the same note names. For instance: E on the open 1st string, E on the 12th fret of the 1st string, and E on the 5th fret of the 2nd string. If you start with any note and go through the music alphabet until you get to the letter you started from, you have traveled the distance of one *octave*. The prefix "octa" signifies the number "eight." As you can see, if you start with E and end with E, you have a total of eight tones. On the guitar, the interval of an octave is the distance of 12 half steps, or frets. By counting the frets and cycling through the music alphabet until you return to the starting letter, you can easily arrive at a note that is an octave higher or lower than your starting note. If you count 24 half steps (or 16 tones), you arrive at the note that is *two* octaves above or below the starting note, etc.

For the moment, we will stick to single strings. Let's start with the A note on the 2nd fret of the 3rd string. We'll climb 12 half steps higher to arrive at the octave note. As noted in the diagram, you can, of course, also descend 12 frets to a lower octave.

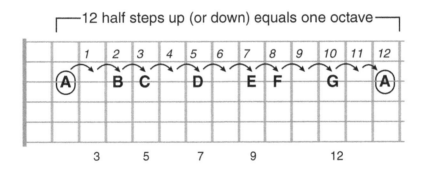

Assignment 6.1

Now it's your turn. In the diagram below, mark the location of the note that is one octave higher than each of the notes indicated. The first one, G, is given. As an additional exercise, find these notes on your guitar (if you have enough frets).

Ex. 1

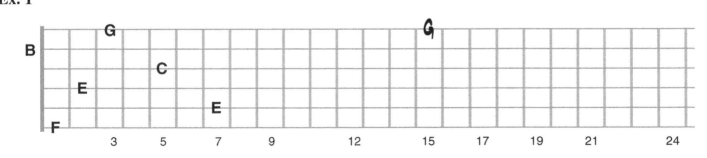

Now mark the location of the note that is one octave *lower* than each of the notes indicated.

Ex. 2

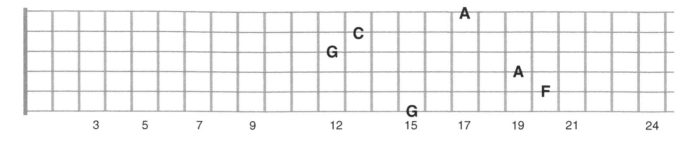

Ear Training 6.1

Octaves have a very unique sound; you can tell that they are the same note, just an octave higher or lower. Try singing "Do–Re–Mi–Fa–Sol–La–Ti–Do," if you are familiar with "Do-Re-Mi" from the musical *The Sound of Music*. When you arrive at the higher "Do," can you hear how that pitch relates to the starting pitch? In essence, octaves sound the same, except they are higher or lower in pitch. It is very useful to familiarize yourself with the sound of the octave.

Track 28 features a series of octaves. Some start with the higher note of the two, and some start with the lower note. Listen to Track 28 and take a moment to let these sounds sink in.

 TRACK 28

UNISONS AND CROSSING STRINGS

The *unison* is the simplest interval because there is no distance between the two notes. A unison consists of two identical pitches with the same name. For instance, the note E (the note for the open 1st string) and the identical note E are unisons. Also, the notes A and A (both on the 3rd string, 2nd fret) are unisons, and so on.

That's the simple part. Now things start to get fun!

On the piano, a unison can only be played in one location. In other words, there is only one key that can be played for each particular pitch. On the guitar, however, there are often several locations where you can choose to play a specific note or pitch. Let's look at our diagram again:

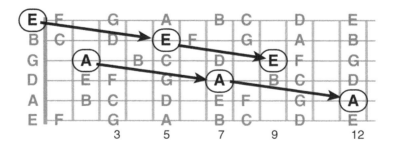

On adjacent strings, the unison for any note on the higher of the two strings can be found on the lower string *five frets up*. This is true of all string pairs except for strings 2 and 3. Here, the unison is *four frets up*. You can see this in the diagram, with the unison Es on the 5th fret of the 2nd string and the 9th fret of the 3rd string. The reason for this exception is because of how the guitar is tuned, but we'll get into that later.

Because the same note can be played in different locations, you can choose what suits you best based on playability and tone. The higher, or thinner, the string you choose, the thinner, brighter, or more *trebly* the tone. As you descend to lower, or thicker, strings, the tone will fatten up and become more bassy. Try playing the notes in the previous diagram, and you will see what we mean.

Assignment 6.2

In the diagram below, mark the location—using the correct note name on the adjacent string—of the unison of each note given.

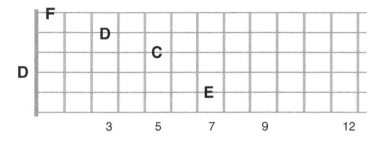

Ear Training 6.2

Track 29 features groups of unisons. For each group, you will first hear the unisons played at the exact same location; then you will hear the unisons played on different strings.

 TRACK 29

Track 30 features six groups of unisons. Some are played in the exact same location on the same string and some are played on different strings. Listen carefully to the tone of each note and determine whether the unisons are played in the same location or on different strings. If they are in the same location, write "same," and if you think they are on different strings, write "different."

TRACK 30

1. _____   3. _____   5. _____

2. _____   4. _____   6. _____

Using Unisons on Different Strings to Tune the Guitar

You may already be able to tune your guitar with an electronic tuner, and that's great! That is a quick way to get the job done while also developing an ear for how the strings are supposed to sound in relation to each other. Now we're going to look at a different way to tune, and it may take a while to get used to, but it's well worth it. In addition to further developing your ear, you will be able to tune when your tuner's batteries die or you don't have any other device available, such as a computer or even your smart phone. Also, you will be able to tune to other musicians who may not be tuned exactly to the pitches of a tuner.

This method, which utilizes unisons on different strings, is called *relative tuning* because you are tuning each string in relation to the string that precedes it. So, even if the guitar is not tuned to *A440* (the A note above *middle C*, which has a frequency of 440 Hz [hertz] and is considered a standard pitch to tune by), your guitar will be in tune with itself because all of the strings are tuned in relation to each other. Sometimes, even entire bands (Green Day, U2, etc.) will tune their instruments down a half step or more.

Refer to the diagram below when following the relative tuning steps beneath it.

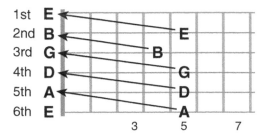

1st E
2nd B
3rd G
4th D
5th A
6th E

E
B
G
D
A

3   5   7

1. Tune your 6th (low E) string to its correct E pitch by using a keyboard, another guitar, an online tuner, or some other device, such as a pitch pipe. (On a keyboard, this pitch is found 12 white keys below middle C.) If you don't have any of these, just approximate the note as best as you can.

2. Play the A note located at the 5th fret of the 6th string, then play A on the open 5th string. These pitches should match; in other words, they are supposed to be unisons. If the 5th string sounds too low, raise the pitch by using the appropriate tuning peg. If it sounds too high, lower the pitch.

3. Play the D note located at the 5th fret of the 5th string, then play the D note on the open 4th string. Match the pitches by adjusting your 4th string as needed.

4. Play the G at the 5th fret of the 4th string, then play the G on the open 3rd string. Match the pitches by adjusting your 3rd string if necessary.

5. We momentarily go out of position for this one (and this is why the unisons on adjacent strings are four frets apart rather than five). Play the B at the 4th fret of the 3rd string, then play B on the open 2nd string. Match the pitches by adjusting your 2nd string if necessary.

6. Finally, play the E on the 5th fret of the 2nd string, then play the E on the open 1st string. Match the pitches by adjusting your 1st string if necessary. You should now be in tune.

Relative tuning takes practice to master, but you possess all the tools. You have done some ear training to recognize higher and lower pitches, as well as recognizing what unisons are supposed to sound like.

Here's a tip: If you feel vibrations throughout the guitar when you are playing the unisons, they are not in tune. If they are really out of tune, the vibrations will be slower and deeper; as you approach the correct pitch, the vibrations will speed up, become smaller, and eventually stop when the pitches match each other perfectly.

Ear Training 6.3

Track 31 walks you through the process of tuning the guitar so you can hear the thought process and adjustments being made.

 TRACK 31

Tuning Quiz

Listen to the following tracks and write down if you think the second tuning note is **higher** than, **lower** than, or **in tune** with the first.

 TRACK 32

1. Is the open 5th-string A (second note) **higher** than, **lower** than, or **in tune** with the 6th-string A (first note)?

_____

 TRACK 33

2. Is the open 4th-string D (second note) **higher** than, **lower** than, or **in tune** with the 5th-string D (first note)?

_____

3. Is the open 3rd-string G (second note) **higher** than, **lower** than, or **in tune** with the 4th-string G (first note)?

_____

4. Is the open 2nd-string B (second note) **higher** than, **lower** than, or **in tune** with the 3rd-string B (first note)?

_____

5. Is the open 1st-string E (second note) **higher** than, **lower** than, or **in tune** with the 2nd-string E (first note)?

_____

OCTAVES ON DIFFERENT STRINGS

So far in this chapter, we've discussed octaves on a single string, unisons on a single string, and unisons on different strings. Now we'll look at a slightly trickier concept: octaves on different strings.

Look back at our diagram of the natural notes on the fretboard.

Using the concepts that we have covered so far in this chapter, we can recognize and understand octaves on different strings. Let's look at the note E on the open 6th string. If we ascend the music alphabet to the note A, we arrive at the 5th fret. We know that A on the 5th fret of the 6th string is the same as A on the open 5th string, so let's cross over to the open 5th string. Now let's climb the music alphabet to D, which brings us to the 5th fret. We know that D on the 5th fret of the 5th string is the same as D on the open 4th string, so let's cross over to the open 4th string. Now let's ascend the 4th string to E, which happens to be the next note. This E is eight notes—and 12 half steps—higher than the E we started on (i.e., one octave higher). Interestingly, if we look at the lower, adjacent string and go five frets higher, you get the unison of the octave E.

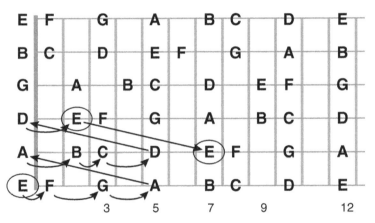

Of course, as we proceed through the music alphabet, we can skip the unisons and just cross over to the next string, like this:

1. 6th string: E–F–G

2. 5th string: A–B–C

3. 4th string: D–E

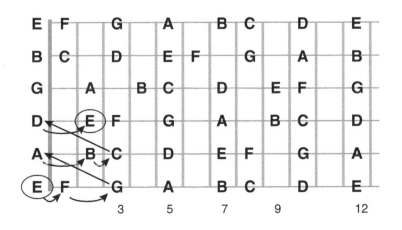

If we continue to apply this concept from the E on the 4th string to the E on the open 1st string, we have gone up one more octave.

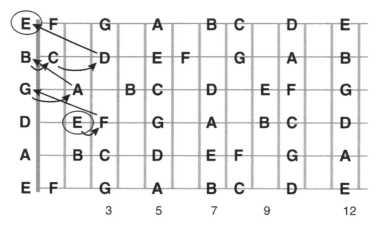

Fretboard Positions

A *position* on the fretboard signifies a four-fret area in which the 1st finger is located at the 1st fret of the position, the 2nd finger at the 2nd fret, etc. So first position indicates frets 1–4, wherein the 1st finger is assigned to the 1st fret (open position and first position are basically the same, except the term "open" implies the use of open strings). Second position consists of frets 2–5, wherein the 1st finger is assigned to the 2nd fret, the 2nd finger is assigned to the 3rd fret, and so on. Third position consists of frets 3–6, wherein the 1st finger is located at the 3rd fret, etc.

The previous examples were in first, or open, position. Let's look at an example in a different position to demonstrate that the concept is the same.

Starting with A on the 5th fret of the 6th string, let's go up one octave while remaining in fifth position. If you follow the process already laid out, you will do the following:

1. 6th string: A–B–C

2. 5th string: D–E–F

3. 4th string: G–A

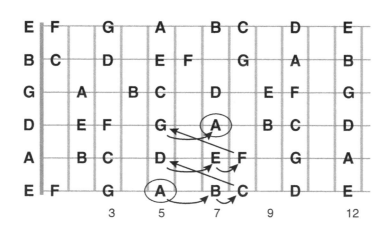

Assignment 6.3

In the diagram below, mark the location (with the correct note name) of the note that is one octave higher than each of the notes indicated. Be sure to stay in the same position of each note given.

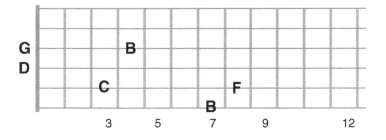

DISTINGUISHING OCTAVES FROM UNISONS

Unisons and octaves have the same note names and sound a lot alike. It is fairly easy to distinguish between the two but can sometimes be a little tricky. Remember: unisons have the exact same pitch, while octaves sound the same, but one of the notes is noticeably higher or lower than the other.

Ear Training 6.4

In Track 37, you will hear comparisons between unisons and octaves so you can get a feel for the unique sound of each.

 TRACK 37

Track 38 features several pitch pairs. In the spaces below, write whether you think the pitches are **unisons** or **octaves**.

 TRACK 38

1. _____   3. _____   5. _____

2. _____   4. _____   6. _____

Chapter 7: ACCIDENTALS AND THE CHROMATIC SCALE

An *accidental* is a symbol used to raise a pitch, lower a pitch, or restore a pitch to its natural state. Accidentals are placed immediately in front of the note that it alters. Accidentals for line notes are centered on the line, and accidentals for space notes are centered in the space (see examples below). We will look at five accidentals: the *sharp*, the *flat*, the *natural*, the *double sharp*, and the *double flat*.

SHARP (♯)

A *sharp* raises a note by one half step. For instance, if a sharp is placed in front of an F note played on the 1st fret of the 1st string, the note becomes F♯ (or F *sharp*) and is played on the 2nd fret of the 1st string. Likewise, if a sharp is placed in front of an A note played on the 2nd fret of the 3rd string, the note becomes A♯ (or A *sharp*) and is played on the 3rd fret of the 3rd string. Let's look at one more: if a sharp is placed in front of a D note played on the open 4th string, the note becomes D♯ (or D *sharp*) and is played on the 1st fret of the 4th string.

TRACK 39

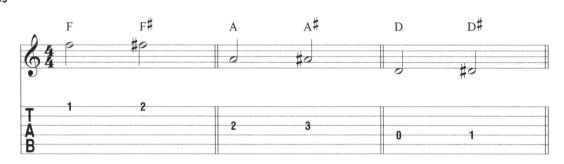

Assignment 7.1

In the examples below, turn each of the given notes into a sharp note. Be sure to include the name of the note on the line, add the sharp to the notation, and show in the tab where the sharp note should be played. For this exercise, keep the sharp note on the same string as the natural note. The first example has been done for you.

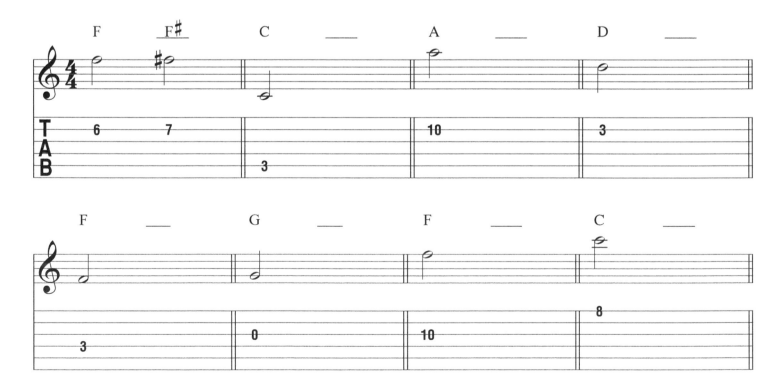

FLAT (♭)

A flat lowers a note by one half step. For example, if a flat is placed in front of an A note played on the 2nd fret of the 3rd string, the note becomes A♭ (or A *flat*) and is played on the 1st fret of the 3rd string. Likewise, if a flat is placed in front of a G note played on the 3rd fret of the 1st string, the note becomes G♭ (or G *flat*) and is played on the 2nd fret of the 1st string. Now, to flat a note that is on an open string, we have to cross to the string immediately below the original string because we can't go any lower on an open string. For example, if a flat is placed in front of an E note played on the open 1st string, the note becomes E♭ (or E *flat*) and is played on the 4th fret of the 2nd string (keep in mind that the original E note could be played on the 5th fret of the 2nd string). Similarly, if a flat is placed in front of an A note played on the open 5th string, the note becomes A♭ (or A *flat*) and is played on the 4th fret of the 6th string.

TRACK 40

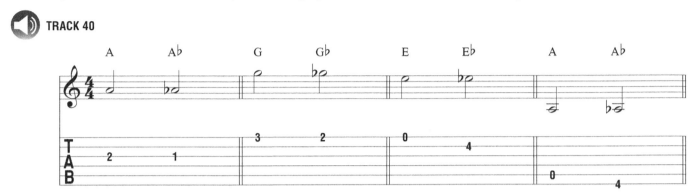

Assignment 7.2

In the examples below, turn each of the given notes into a flat note. Be sure to include the name of the note on the line, add the flat to the notation, and show in the tab where the flat note should be played. For this exercise, keep the flat note on the same string as the natural note, except when the natural note is on an open string. The first example has been done for you.

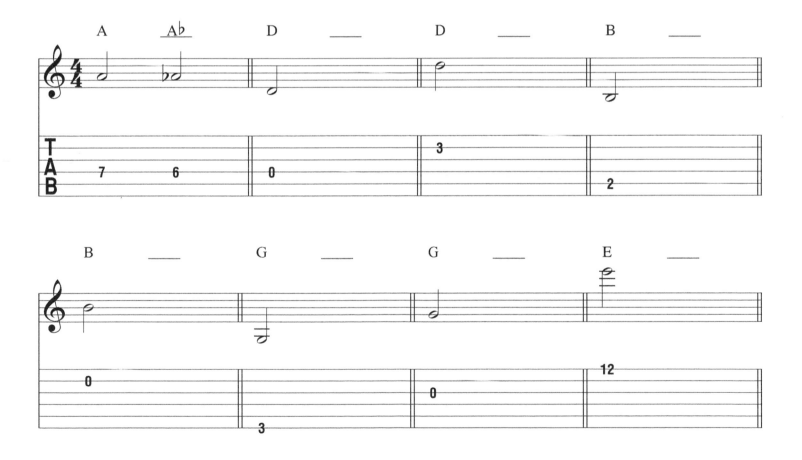

NATURAL (♮)

A *natural* sign returns an altered note to its natural, or original, location. For example, if we encounter an A# on the 3rd fret of the 3rd string, followed by an A with a natural sign in front of it, the new note is A♮ (or A *natural*) and is played on the 2nd fret of the 3rd string. Similarly, if we see a D♭ on the 2nd fret of the 2nd string, followed by a D with a natural sign in front of it, the new note is D♮ (or D *natural*) and is played on the 3rd fret of the 2nd string.

Let's look at two more examples: if a C# located at the 9th fret of the 1st string is followed by a C with a natural sign in front of it, the new note is C♮ (or C *natural*) and is played on the 8th fret of the 1st string. Finally, if a D♭ located on the 4th fret of the 5th string is followed by a D with a natural sign in front of it, the new note is D♮ (or D *natural*) and is played on the open 4th string (or the 5th fret of the 5th string).

TRACK 41

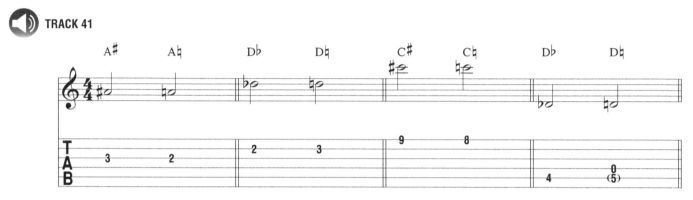

Assignment 7.3

In the examples below, turn each of the given altered notes into a natural note. Be sure to include the name of the note on the line, add the natural sign to the notation, and show in the tab where the natural note should be played. For this exercise, keep the natural note on the same string as the altered note, except when the natural note can be played on an open string. The first example has been done for you.

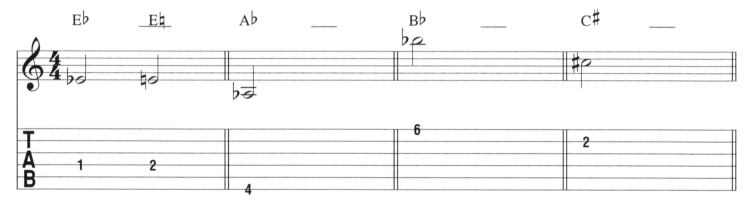

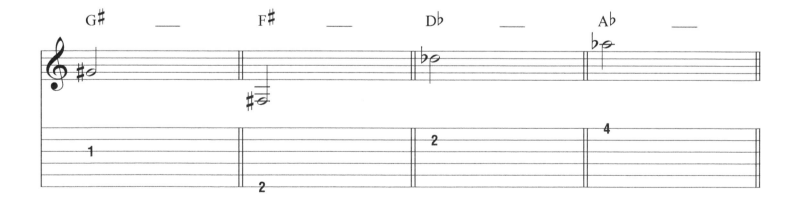

42

DOUBLE SHARPS (✗) AND DOUBLE FLATS (♭♭)

Double sharps and *double flats* appear less often than regular sharps and flats, but you will encounter them occasionally.

A *double sharp* raises a note by two half steps, or one whole step. So, if a double sharp is placed in front of an E note played on the 2nd fret of the 4th string, the note becomes E✗ (or E *double sharp*) and is played on the 4th fret of the 4th string. Likewise, C✗ can be played on the 3rd fret of the 2nd string and G✗ can be played on the 2nd fret of the 3rd string, as shown below:

TRACK 42

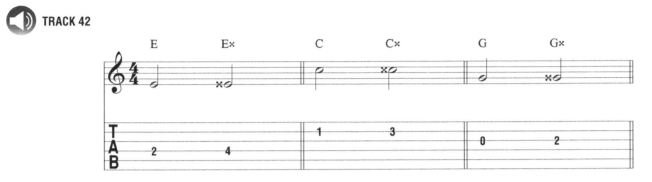

A *double flat* lowers a note by two half steps, or one whole step. So, if a double flat is placed in front of an F note played on the 3rd fret of the 4th string, the note becomes F♭♭ (or F *double flat*) and is played on the 1st fret of the 4th string. If a double flat is placed in front of the G note played on the open 3rd string, we can cross to the next, lower string and go down two frets (starting from the 5th fret) to play G♭♭ on the 3rd fret of the 4th string. In addition, if we place a double flat in front of the C played on the 1st fret of the 2nd string, we can cross to the next, lower string and go down two frets (starting from the 5th fret) to play C♭♭ on the 3rd fret of the 3rd string.

TRACK 43

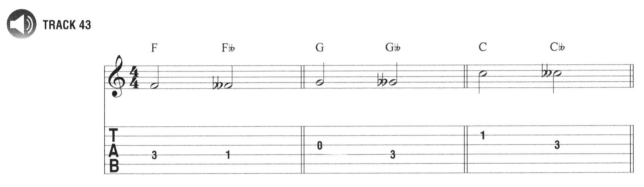

Assignment 7.4

In the examples below, alter each of the given notes with either a double sharp or a double flat as indicated. Be sure to include the name of the note on the line, add the accidental to the notation, and show in the tab where the altered note should be played. For this exercise, keep the altered note on the same string as the natural note, except when the natural note is on an open string and you are altering it with a double flat. The first answer is provided for you.

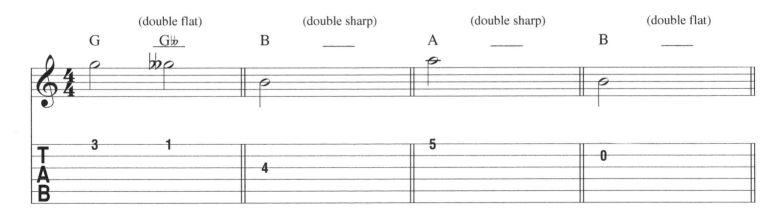

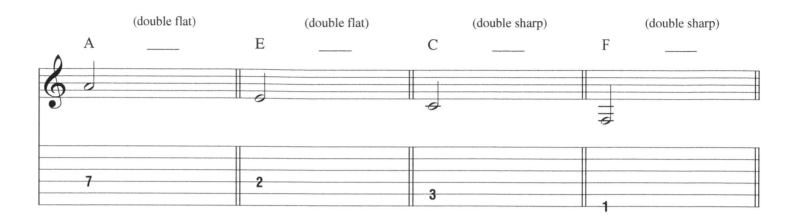

RULES FOR ACCIDENTALS

Unless it is cancelled by another accidental, an accidental is in effect for the entire measure in which it appears. Additionally, if an altered note is tied and carried over to another measure, the accidental is in effect for the new measure, as well (unless otherwise cancelled).

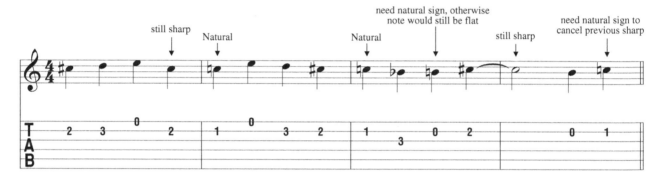

Accidentals only apply to the octaves in which they appear.

Courtesy accidentals sometimes appear in parentheses and are used to clarify or make the music easier to read. A courtesy accidental can be used as a reminder for the rules above. (**Note:** After this example, this book will not use parentheses for courtesy accidentals.)

Assignment 7.5

Using open (or first) position, write the locations of the standard notation notes by filling in their corresponding tab numbers.

ENHARMONIC EQUIVALENTS AND ACCIDENTALS ON THE FRETBOARD

Every flat note can also be referred to as a sharp note. When two notes have the exact same pitch but different names, they are *enharmonic equivalents*. Let's listen to a few examples:

 TRACK 44

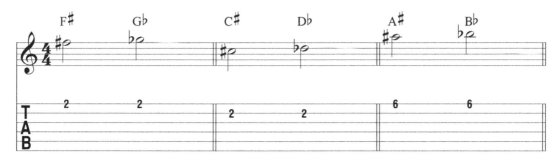

As you can tell from the recording, though these notes are written differently, they have the exact same sound.

For a visual display of enharmonic equivalents on the fretboard, let's look at a diagram with all the sharp and flat notes added to the natural notes. Every fret that has a sharp name and a flat name is the location of an enharmonic equivalent.

E	F	F♯/G♭	G	G♯/A♭	A	A♯/B♭	B	C	C♯/D♭	D	D♯/E♭	E
B	C	C♯/D♭	D	D♯/E♭	E	F	F♯/G♭	G	G♯/A♭	A	A♯/B♭	B
G	G♯/A♭	A	A♯/B♭	B	C	C♯/D♭	D	D♯/E♭	E	F	F♯/G♭	G
D	D♯/E♭	E	F	F♯/G♭	G	G♯/A♭	A	A♯/B♭	B	C	C♯/D♭	D
A	A♯/B♭	B	C	C♯/D♭	D	D♯/E♭	E	F	F♯/G♭	G	G♯/A♭	A
E	F	F♯/G♭	G	G♯/A♭	A	A♯/B♭	B	C	C♯/D♭	D	D♯/E♭	E
		3		5		7		9				12

Above, you have a diagram showing all the notes on the fretboard up to the 12th fret. From our discussion about octaves, you know that all the notes start over at the 12th fret. Therefore, you now know all the notes on the fretboard!

Another, trickier instance of enharmonic equivalents involves double sharps and double flats. For instance, F𝄪 requires us to raise the pitch F by two half steps, which brings us to the note G, so F𝄪 and G are enharmonic equivalents. Likewise, for D♭♭, we have to lower the pitch D by two half steps, which brings us to the note C, so D♭♭ and C are enharmonic equivalents.

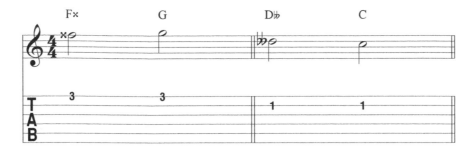

As with the example above, there are even instances in which a note with a single sharp or flat can be enharmonically equivalent to a natural note:

 TRACK 46

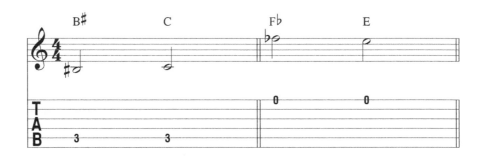

You may be thinking: how do I know which note name to say or use? For now, don't worry about it. There are certain guidelines, but we won't get into them until later in the book.

Assignment 7.6

For this exercise, the tab indicates the locations for pairs of enharmonic equivalents. Notate the enharmonic equivalents in the standard notation staff and write the note names in the lines above the staff. The first pair of enharmonic equivalents has been done for you.

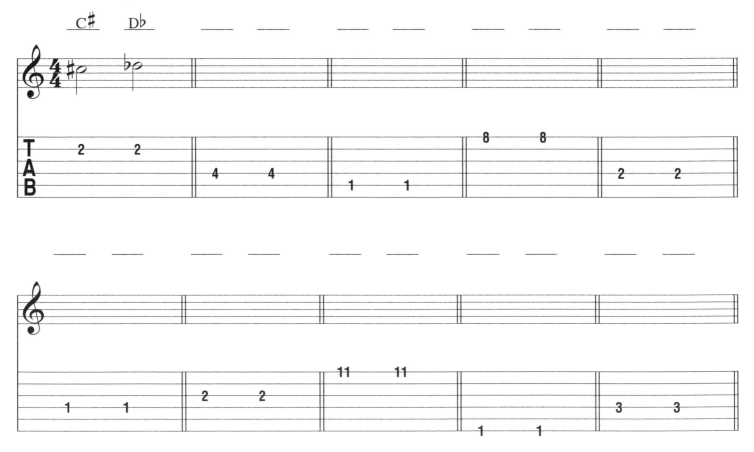

Assignment 7.7

Below is a selection of sharp and flat notes on strings 1–6. In the diagram that follows, write the note names in the correct locations on the indicated strings.

1. 1st string: G#, E♭
2. 2nd string: D♭, F#
3. 3rd string: A♭, G
4. 4th string: F♭, B♭
5. 5th string: B#, E#
6. 6th string: C♭, C𝄪

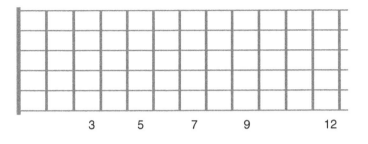

THE CHROMATIC SCALE

Now that you know all of the sharp notes, flat notes, and enharmonic equivalents, we can look at the *chromatic scale*. First of all, a *scale* is an arrangement of notes that progresses through the music alphabet and has a set pattern of half steps and whole steps. The term *chromatic* means movement in half steps. So the chromatic scale is a scale made up entirely of half steps—12 half steps from the starting note, or *tonic*. You can begin with any note on the fretboard and end on the same note an octave higher. This would be an *ascending* version of the scale, which uses sharp notes. For instance:

TRACK 47

A *descending* (downward moving) version of the scale would use flat notes (you can see where enharmonic equivalents come into play).

TRACK 48

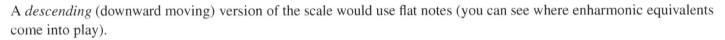

Let's start with a different note, G.

TRACK 49

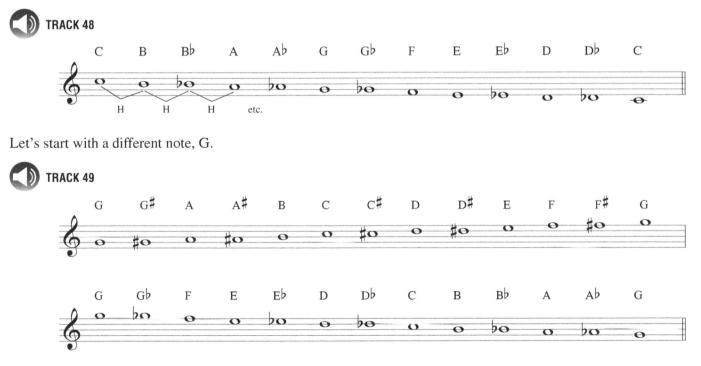

The Chromatic Scale on a Single String

The chromatic scale can be easily visualized and played on a single string. If you start with an open string and ascend in half steps until you arrive at the octave on the 12th fret, you have played an ascending chromatic scale. Likewise, if you descend from the 12th fret in half steps until you reach the open string, you have played a descending chromatic scale.

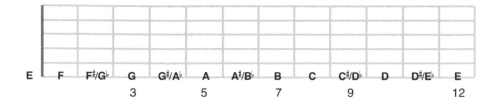

You can also start on any fret of any string and ascend/descend 12 half steps to play a chromatic scale. For example, let's start with F on the 3rd fret of the 4th string:

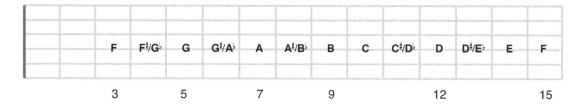

The Chromatic Scale Crossing Strings

Instead of the linear, or horizontal, approach to playing the chromatic scale on a single string, we can cross strings for a more vertical approach. As an example, let's start with the E note on the open 6th string and go up an octave to the E on the 2nd fret of the 4th string, all while staying in first (open) position. Below are the notes on a fretboard diagram, and then in standard notation and tab.

E Chromatic Scale

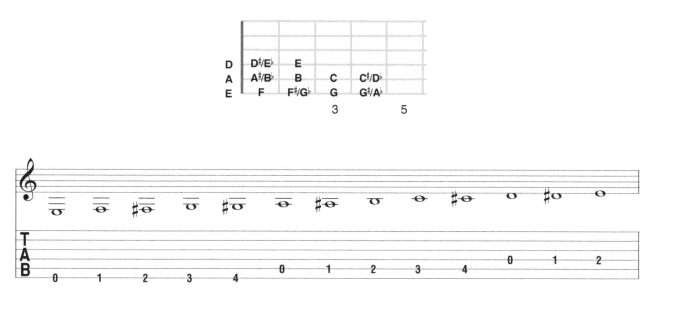

We can start on any note and cross strings for a vertical approach. Let's start with the F note on the 3rd fret of the 4th string:

F Chromatic Scale

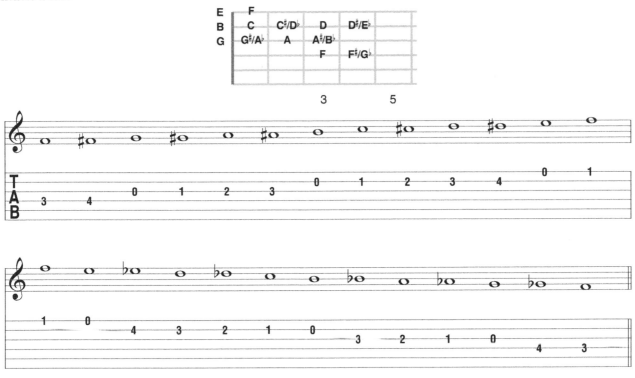

Assignment 7.8

1. Notate an ascending chromatic scale starting with the note given. Include note names on the blanks.

2. Notate a descending chromatic scale starting with the note given. Include note names on the blanks.

3. Using the correct note names (including enharmonic equivalents), show a chromatic scale on a single string, starting with the D note on the open 4th string.

4. Using the correct note names (including enharmonic equivalents), show a chromatic scale on a single string, starting with the C note on the 1st fret of the 2nd string.

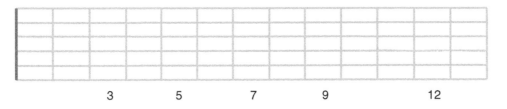

49

5a. Using the correct note names (including enharmonic equivalents), show a chromatic scale crossing strings, starting with the F note on the 3rd fret of the 4th string.

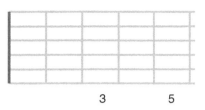

3   5

5b. Notate the F chromatic scale above in the standard notation and tab staffs (or *staves*) below. Include note names in the blanks provided.

Ascending

F

Descending

Chapter 8: THE MAJOR SCALE

Remember, in the previous chapter, a *scale* was defined as a series of notes in a particular arrangement of half steps and whole steps. There are many different types of scales, the most important of which, at least in terms of music theory, is the *major scale*. All other scales can be defined by comparing them to the major scale.

The major scale has a recognizable sound and is often identified by the *solfège* syllables: Do–Re–Mi–Fa–Sol–La–Ti–Do. Notice that there are seven syllables (the first is repeated at the end); the major scale contains seven notes that can be expressed with solfège or indicated with numbers known as *scale degrees* (1–2–3–4–5–6–7–8). (**Note:** Scale degree "8" is the octave of scale degree "1.") The first note of the scale, the note upon which the scale is built, is the *tonic*. The note names always cycle consecutively through the music alphabet, depending on which letter you start with; for example, the C major scale would be: C–D–E–F–G–A–B–C.

Below is the C major scale, which has no sharps or flats. The note names and scale degrees are indicated.

C Major Scale

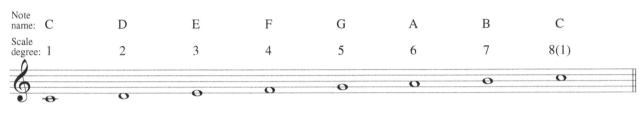

THE MAJOR SCALE FORMULA

Every major scale is constructed from the same formula of whole steps and half steps. In the example below, you will see that this formula is: whole–whole–half–whole–whole–whole–half. We'll use "W" to indicate whole step and "H" to indicate half step. Note that the distances between scale degrees are whole steps, except between scale degrees 3 and 4 and 7 and 8.

🔊 TRACK 50

C Major Scale

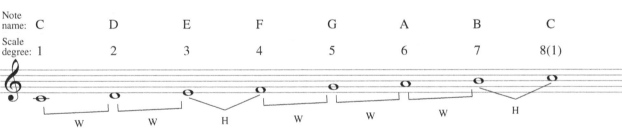

If we start from any note and follow the major scale formula above, the result will be another major scale whose letter name is the same as the starting note. Some scales will require sharps to maintain the scale formula, and some will require flats. Let's look at some examples.

If we start with a G note and make our way through the music alphabet, we get the following:

TRACK 51

G Major Scale

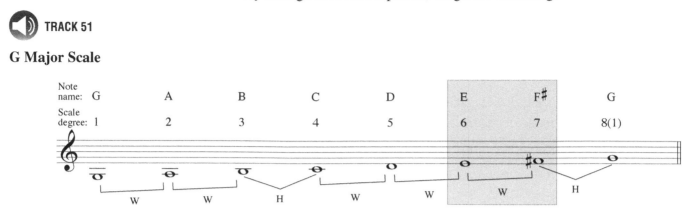

Notice above that, in order to maintain the required whole step between E and F#, we needed to sharp the F.

Note: Major scales consist of the same notes when ascending and descending, so the G major scale would use an F# when going up *and* when going down.

Below is another scale that uses sharps to maintain the major scale formula. This one starts with a D note and requires us to sharp the F and C notes to maintain the pattern.

TRACK 52

D Major Scale

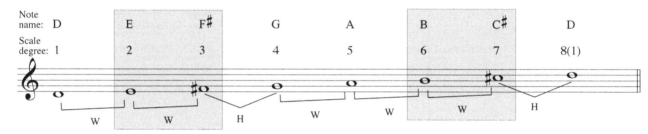

Below is a major scale built on the note F, and it presents a slightly different situation. For this scale, we have to flat the B to preserve the half step between the 3rd and 4th scale degrees.

TRACK 53

F Major Scale

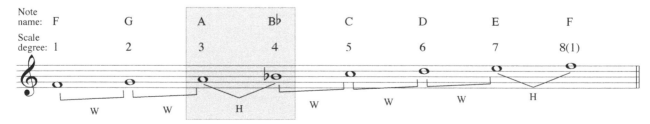

We'll look at one more, this time with a B♭ tonic. Coincidentally, we need to flat the 4th scale degree for this one, as well.

🔊 **TRACK 54**

B♭ Major Scale

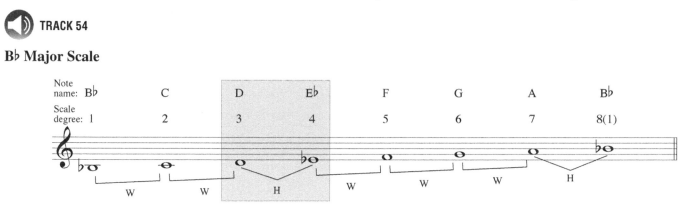

Because there are 15 possible notes (including enharmonic equivalents), there are 15 possible major scales. They can be divided into the following categories:

Natural Scale (no sharps or flats)	Sharp Scales	Flat Scales
C Major	G Major (1 sharp)	F Major (1 flat)
	D Major (2 sharps)	B♭ Major (2 flats)
	A Major (3 sharps)	E♭ Major (3 flats)
	E Major (4 sharps)	A♭ Major (4 flats)
	B Major (5 sharps)	D♭ Major (5 flats)
	F♯ Major (6 sharps)	G♭ Major (6 flats)
	C♯ Major (7 sharps)	C♭ Major (7 flats)

Later in the book, you will see why the scales proceed in the order listed above.

An important thing to remember is that a single major scale may use sharps or flats, but never together in the same scale.

Assignment 8.1

In the following examples, notate the major scales that start with the tonics provided. Figure out the correct notes by applying the step pattern covered on the previous pages. Write the notes in the standard notation staff. Also, fill in the correct note names and scale degrees in the blanks above the staff. (You can tell if you have the right number of sharps or flats in each scale by referring to the list of sharp scales and flat scales.)

1.

2.

3.

Note
name: E♭

Scale
degree: 1

4.

Note
name: A♭

Scale
degree: 1

THE MAJOR SCALE ON A SINGLE STRING

By looking at the major scale on a single string, we get a great representation of the step pattern laid out in a linear fashion across the fretboard. It can make understanding the major scale easy. Let's begin by looking at the E major scale, starting with the open 1st string. Follow the W–W–H–W–W–W–H pattern all the way up the string to the octave E at the 12th fret.

E Major Scale

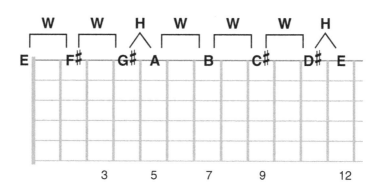

Remember: you can start with any note, on any fret. Let's begin with F on the 3rd fret of the 4th string and follow the step pattern up to the octave F on the 15th fret.

F Major Scale

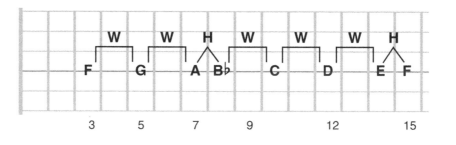

As you can see, the single-string major scale makes it very easy to visualize and understand the step pattern on the fretboard. Also, it can help you figure out all the notes of any major scale.

Assignment 8.2

Using the tonics provided in the following diagrams, write the correct note names in their correct locations to construct single-string major scales.

1.

2.

3.

4.

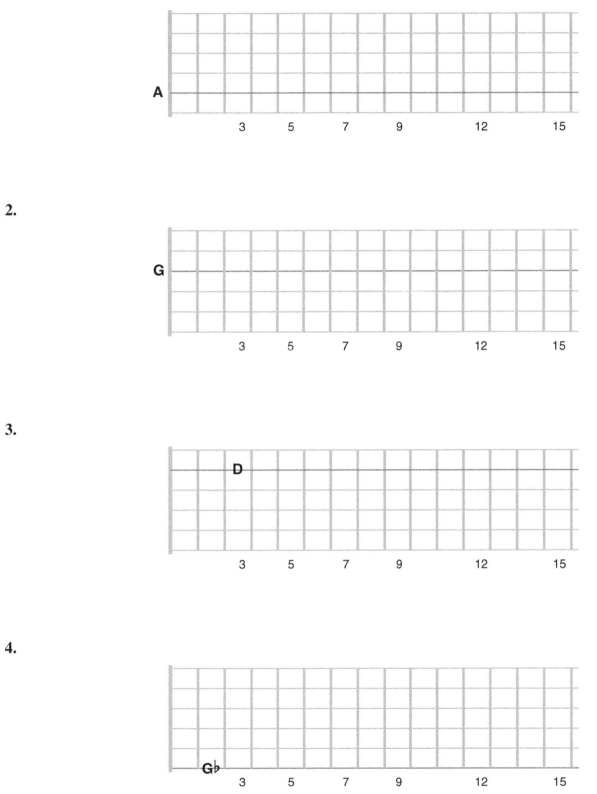

THE MAJOR SCALE CROSSING STRINGS

As you may have found in the previous section, playing a major scale on a single string is a bit awkward—especially if you want to play it with any kind of speed. So, in this section, we'll look at how to play major scales by crossing strings.

Open Position

If you remember from earlier in the book, open position is in first position (frets 1–4) and utilizes open strings. It takes a little more work to apply the major scale step formula when crossing strings.

Remember:

- From the 4th fret of one string to the next higher open string is the distance of a **half step**. This is true for all string pairs except from the 3rd to the 2nd, in which case, a half step occurs from the 3rd fret of one string to the next higher open string.

- From the 3rd fret of one string to the next higher open string is the distance of a **whole step**. This is true for all string pairs except from the 3rd to the 2nd, in which case, a whole step occurs from the 2nd fret of one string to the next higher open string.

Let's look at the C major scale with an open-position fingering:

C Major Scale (Open Position)

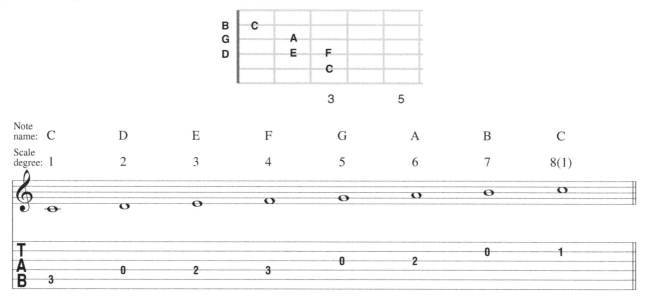

Now let's look at the F major scale with an open-position fingering:

F Major Scale (Open Position)

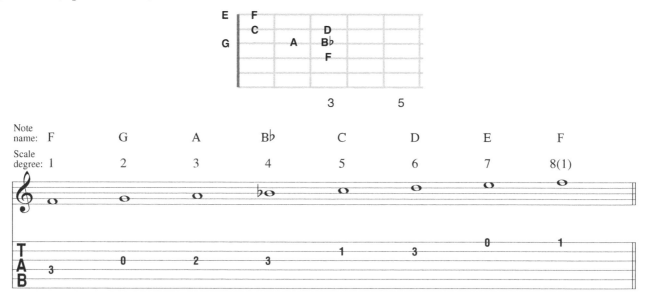

Assignment 8.3

1a. In the diagram below, use the correct note names to construct an open-position G major scale that crosses strings and begins with the G on the open 3rd string.

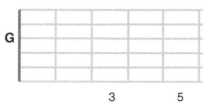

1b. Notate the G major scale from **1a** in the standard notation and tab staffs below. Include note names and scale degrees in the blanks provided.

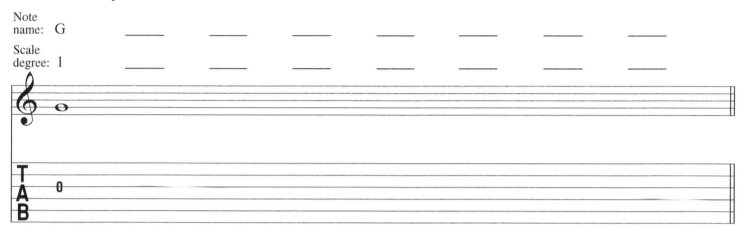

2a. In the diagram below, use the correct note names to construct an open-position E major scale that crosses strings and begins with the E on the 2nd fret of the 4th string.

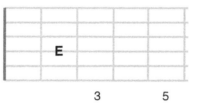

2b. Notate the E major scale above in the standard notation and tab staffs below. Include note names and scale degrees in the blanks provided.

Closed Position (Moveable Scale Forms)

Now we have come to one of the wonderful and efficient aspects of the guitar. On many other instruments, you need to learn a different fingering for each different scale, or *key* (we'll cover keys in the next chapter). But, on the guitar, if you know one fingering, you know 15 major scales. By avoiding open strings, we can use *closed*, or *moveable*, scale forms. A moveable form can be relocated anywhere on the fretboard, and the type, or quality, of the scale will remain the same—only the pitch range and letter name of the scale will change. Let's look at an example.

The following is the G major scale using the crossing-strings approach, but without any open strings. This scale is in second position, because our 1st finger is located at the 2nd fret and we are covering frets 2–5.

G Major Scale (Moveable Form)

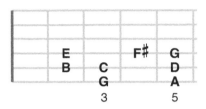

You can see that the scale starts with the G note on the 3rd fret of the 6th string. If we move the scale up two frets so that it starts with A on the 5th fret of the 6th string, we have the A major scale.

A Major Scale (Moveable Form)

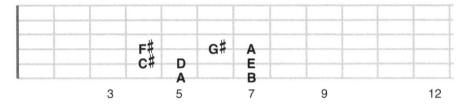

As you can see, the fingering remains the same—only the note names change. Wherever you move the scale form, it stays major in quality, but with a new letter name. If we moved the first note to the 8th fret, we would have the C major scale; if we start at the 10th fret, we would have the D major scale; and so on.

Note: There are other moveable fingerings you could come up with. If you feel you have a solid understanding of this concept, try coming up with a couple of your own.

Assignment 8.4

1. In the diagram below, use the correct note names to construct a closed-position (moveable) D major scale that crosses strings and begins with the D on the 10th fret of the 6th string. (Apply the same form as discussed above.)

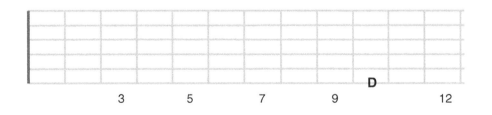

2. In the diagram below, use the correct note names to construct a closed-position (moveable) B♭ major scale that crosses strings and begins with the B♭ on the 6th fret of the 6th string. (Again, apply the same form as discussed above.)

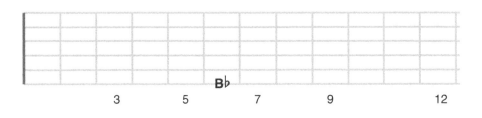

The purpose of this ear-training exercise is to really get the sound of the major scale into your ear.

In Track 55, you will hear a couple of major scales, each starting with a different tonic. Listen to them several times to really absorb the feel and sound.

 TRACK 55

Quiz

Listen to the following tracks. In each case, you will hear a scale. First, decide whether or not it is a major scale played correctly. If it is, mark "yes" in the first blank, and if it is not, write "no." If your answer is "no," write in the second blank which scale degree is played incorrectly (there will only be one wrong note). Listen to each track as many times as it takes for you to get the correct answer. Good luck!

Yes/No   Incorrect Scale Degree

🎵 **TRACK 56**

1. _____   _____

🎵 **TRACK 57**

2. _____   _____

🎵 **TRACK 58**

3. _____   _____

🎵 **TRACK 59**

4. _____   _____

🎵 **TRACK 60**

5. _____   _____

🎵 **TRACK 61**

6. _____   _____

🎵 **TRACK 62**

7. _____   _____

🔊 **TRACK 63**

8. _____   _____

Chapter 9: KEYS, KEY SIGNATURES, AND THE CIRCLE OF 5THS

KEYS

A *key* is the tonal center of a piece of music. The notes of a major scale make up the notes of a major key with the same name. Both the scale and the key are named for the tonic note. For instance, the notes of the C major scale constitute the key of C major. There are no sharps or flats in the C major scale, so there are no sharps or flats in the key of C major, or simply, the "key of C."

KEY SIGNATURES

A *key signature* is present at the beginning of every piece of music, and it indicates the key by showing how many sharps or flats are in the piece. For example, let's look at an A major scale:

Instead of inserting a sharp to the left of every C, F, and G note, we use a key signature:

The accidentals in the key signature remain in effect *for all octaves* throughout the piece unless altered by a natural sign (♮).

Assignment 9.1

In the following examples, write the corresponding tab—in open position—for the standard notation.

Remember to refer to the key signature to see which notes are sharp or flat throughout the example (unless otherwise altered by a natural sign).

1.

2.

3.

4.

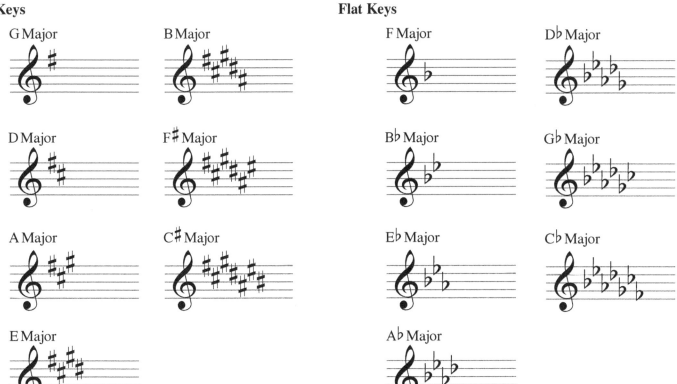

Below are all of the major key signatures. (Remember: the key of C major has no sharps or flats.)

Sharp Keys   **Flat Keys**

G Major   B Major   F Major   D♭ Major

D Major   F♯ Major   B♭ Major   G♭ Major

A Major   C♯ Major   E♭ Major   C♭ Major

E Major   A♭ Major

Tips for Figuring Out What Key You're In

- **For sharp keys:** Take the last sharp, the one all the way to the right, raise it up a half step, and that is your key. For instance, look at the key signature with four sharps. The sharp all the way to the right is D♯. Raise D♯ a half step and you get E. So, the key with four sharps is E major.

- **For flat keys:** First, you need to remember that the key of F has one flat, B♭. But after that, it's easy to figure out the flat keys. The second-to-last flat tells you the key. For example, if you look at the key with four flats, you'll see that the second-to-last flat is A♭. The key with four flats is the key of A♭ major.

The good news is, you won't come across *all* of these keys when reading guitar music, but eventually, you will encounter quite a few of them.

Assignment 9.2

Using the tips from the previous section, figure out the following key signatures. Write your answers in the blanks.

1. _____

2. _____

3. _____

4. _____

5. _____

6. _____

7. _____

8. _____

9. _____

10. _____

11. _____

12. _____

13. _____

14. _____

15. _____

CIRCLE OF 5THS

A helpful system for organizing and remembering keys and key signatures is the *circle of 5ths*. (**Note:** A *5th* is the distance between the tonic and 5th degree of a scale.) Check out the following diagram:

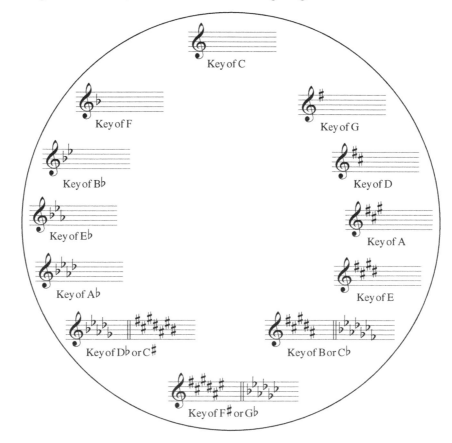

At the top of the circle of 5ths is C major, which has no sharps or flats. From that point, if we travel clockwise around the circle, we get the sharp keys. If we go up a 5th from C (C–D–E–F–G), we get G. If we go up a 5th from G (G–A–B–C–D), we get D, etc. Each time we go up a 5th, we add a sharp to the key signature, and that sharp is always the 7th of that key. In addition, each new sharp is a 5th above the previous sharp (F♯, C♯, G♯, D♯, etc.). By applying this information, you could write out a key signature with any number of sharps without first knowing the name of the key. For instance, if you were told to write out a key signature with four sharps, you would start with F♯ and then count up in 5ths from there: F♯–C♯–G♯–D♯. Raise the last sharp a half step, and you'll find that you are in the key of E major.

If we start from C and proceed counterclockwise around the circle, we get the flat keys. However, in this direction, each new key is a *4th* higher than the previous one. (**Note:** A 4th is the distance between the tonic and 4th degree of a scale.) From C to F is a 4th (C–D–E–F), from F to B♭ is a 4th (F–G–A–B♭), etc. In this direction, we add a flat to each new key signature, and that flat is always the 4th of that key. In addition, each new flat is a 4th above the previous flat (B♭, E♭, A♭, D♭, etc.). By applying this information, you could write out a key signature with any number of flats without first knowing the name of the key. For example, if you were told to write out a key signature with four flats, you would start with B♭ and then count up in 4ths from there: B♭, E♭, A♭, and D♭. The second-to-last flat gives us our key, so we are in the key of A♭ major.

Note that C♯ and D♭, G♭ and F♯, and B and C♭ occupy the same points of the circle. This means that they are enharmonic equivalents—the pitches are exactly the same in both keys, but they are spelled with different note names.

Assignment 9.3

Examples 1 and 2 are lists of accidentals for major key signatures. Fill in the missing accidentals.

1. F♯, C♯, _____

2. B♭, _____, A♭

3. What key does Example 1 indicate? _____

4. What key does Example 2 indicate? _____

5. On the staff to the right, write out a key signature with five sharps.

6. On the staff to the right, write out a key signature with five flats.

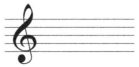

7. On the staff to the right, write out a key signature with six sharps.

8. On the staff to the right, write out a key signature with six flats.

9. What key does Example 5 indicate? _____

10. What key does Example 6 indicate? _____

11. What key does Example 7 indicate? _____

12. What key does Example 8 indicate? _____

Chapter 10: INTERVALS

We've learned that an interval is the distance between two pitches. Examples of intervals are half steps, whole steps, unisons, octaves, 4ths, and 5ths—all of which you now have some experience with. Remember: intervals are determined by counting the note names between two pitches, and that gives us a number. For instance, say we are looking for the interval between C and F:

First, we would count the note names in between those two notes, including the notes themselves:

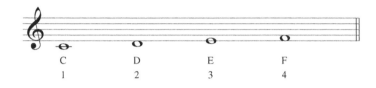

We arrive at the number "4," so our interval is a *4th*.

Intervals also have *qualities*, and there are five types: *major*, *minor*, *perfect*, *augmented*, and *diminished*. For instance, our 4th above is actually a *perfect* 4th. We'll look at the qualities in greater detail later in this chapter.

Additionally, an interval can be *melodic* or *harmonic*. A melodic interval consists of two notes played one after the other, whereas a harmonic interval is comprised of two notes played simultaneously.

INTERVALS OF THE MAJOR SCALE

Intervals of the major scale are determined by the distance between the tonic and the other scale degrees. For example, from the tonic to the second degree of the scale is the interval of a *2nd*, from the tonic to the third degree is a *3rd*, etc. The major scale contains only perfect and major intervals. Below is the C major scale with its intervals labeled. In these examples, we are using open position to play the intervals.

TRACK 64

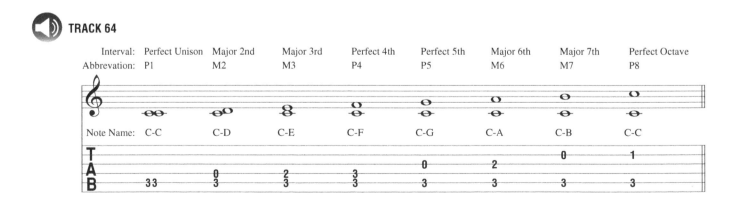

We looked at the major scale intervals played harmonically. To really get the sound of the intervals into our ear, let's also play them melodically.

TRACK 65

The same formula applies to every major scale. Let's look at the intervals of the G major scale below. (**Note:** In order to play the first two intervals harmonically/simultaneously, the roots are voiced at the 5th fret of the 4th string—outside of open position.)

TRACK 66

Interval:	Perfect Unison	Major 2nd	Major 3rd	Perfect 4th	Perfect 5th	Major 6th	Major 7th	Perfect Octave
Abbrevation:	P1	M2	M3	P4	P5	M6	M7	P8
Note Name:	G-G	G-A	G-B	G-C	G-D	G-E	G-F#	G-G

Now let's play through the intervals melodically.

TRACK 67

Here is how the interval qualities break down in a major scale:

Perfect	Major
Unison	2nd
4th	3rd
5th	6th
Octave	7th

Ear Training 10.1

On Track 68, you will hear eight different intervals. Each one has the same tonic, and each one will be played melodically and harmonically. By now, you are comfortable with the sound of the major scale, so when you hear the intervals, hum the scale (while keeping the interval in mind) and try to identify the scale degree. That will give you the interval. This takes practice, so don't be frustrated if it doesn't come easy at first. Remember: the ear is a muscle that needs to be developed.

 TRACK 68

1. _____   5. _____

2. _____   6. _____

3. _____   7. _____

4. _____   8. _____

Let's mix it up a little. Now you will hear a series of intervals that have different tonics. Consider this a challenge. Again, this skill will take time to truly master, but it is invaluable.

 TRACK 69

9. _____   13. _____

10. _____   14. _____

11. _____   15. _____

12. _____   16. _____

MORE ABOUT INTERVAL QUALITIES

Intervals and interval qualities can be measured in whole steps and half steps. For instance, a minor 3rd is the distance of one-and-a-half steps, while a major 3rd is the distance of two whole steps.

Half steps determine interval qualities. Let's look at how this works:

- Lower the top note in a major interval by a half step and you get a minor interval.

 **TRACK 70**

- Raise the top note in a perfect interval by a half step and you get an augmented interval.

 **TRACK 71**

- Lower the top note in a perfect interval by a half step and you get a diminished interval.

 **TRACK 72**

Assignment 10.1

The following examples consist of pairs of intervals. Each interval is labeled. Turn the second interval of each pair into the interval type and quality that is indicated above the staff. Do this by placing one accidental in front of the top note in the second interval. The first one is done for you.

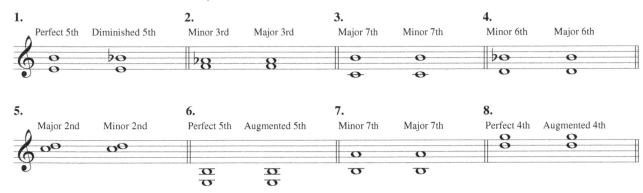

Ear Training 10.2

In Track 73, you will hear a series of interval pairs. The qualities of the two intervals are given below. Write in each blank whether you think that interval quality is played **1st** or **2nd**.

TRACK 73

1. major _____ minor _____

2. major _____ minor _____

3. minor _____ major _____

4. major _____ minor _____

5. diminished _____ minor _____

6. perfect _____ augmented _____

7. augmented _____ perfect _____

8. major _____ minor _____

INTERVALS WITHIN ONE OCTAVE

Below are all of the intervals within one octave—in this case, from C to C. The note names and intervals are indicated, as are abbreviations and distances in steps and half steps. Play each interval harmonically and melodically to accustom your ear to the different-sounding intervals. You will notice some are *consonant* (pleasant sounding), like the major 3rd, and some are *dissonant* (clashing), like the diminished 5th. Also, note that some of these intervals are enharmonic equivalents—namely, the augmented 4th and diminished 5th and the augmented 5th and minor 6th.

TRACK 74

Perfect Unison	Minor 2nd	Major 2nd	Minor 3rd	Major 3rd	Perfect 4th	Augmented 4th
P1	m2	M2	m3	M3	P4	A4
0 steps	1/2 step	1 step	1-1/2 steps	2 steps	2-1/2 steps	3 steps
C-C	C-Db	C-D	C-Eb	C-E	C-F	C-F#

Diminished 5th	Perfect 5th	Augmented 5th	Minor 6th	Major 6th	Minor 7th	Major 7th	Perfect Octave
d5	P5	A5	m6	M6	m7	M7	P8
3 steps	3-1/2 steps	4 steps	4 steps	4-1/2 steps	5 steps	5-1/2 steps	6 steps
C-Gb	C-G	C-G#	C-Ab	C-A	C-Bb	C-B	C-C

TIPS FOR RECOGNIZING INTERVALS

You can use parts of familiar melodies to help you recognize particular intervals. The following is a list of some of these:

- **Minor 2nd:** Opening to the theme from the movie *Jaws*
- **Major 2nd:** Opening to the classic song "You Really Got Me," made famous by the Kinks and Van Halen
- **Minor 3rd:** First two notes in the opening riff to Deep Purple's "Smoke on the Water"
- **Major 3rd:** First couple of notes in "Blister in the Sun" by Violent Femmes
- **Perfect 4th:** The first few notes in the classic wedding piece "Here Comes the Bride"
- **Augmented 4th/Diminished 5th:** The first two notes in *The Simpsons* theme song
- **Perfect 5th:** The intro to "Rikki Don't Lose That Number" by Steely Dan, the first few notes in "When I Come Around" by Green Day, and the first chord in "Lose Yourself" by Eminem
- **Minor 6th:** The second chord in "Lose Yourself" by Eminem, and the first two notes in "Who Are You?" by Black Sabbath
- **Major 6th:** The first two notes in the NBC (National Broadcasting Company) chimes
- **Minor 7th:** First two notes of the *Star Trek* theme, after the spoken intro
- **Major 7th:** First few sung notes in "Don't Know Why" by Norah Jones
- **Perfect octave:** Main riff to "Immigrant Song" by Led Zeppelin

Ear Training 10.3

On Track 75, you will hear a series of intervals played harmonically and melodically. Use the tips mentioned earlier to help you figure out which interval is being played. Remember to hum them, and also try humming the notes in between the interval pitches to determine the correct interval. All of these intervals utilize the same tonic.

🔊 **TRACK 75**

1. _____	6. _____	11. _____
2. _____	7. _____	12. _____
3. _____	8. _____	13. _____
4. _____	9. _____	14. _____
5. _____	10. _____	

On Track 76, you will hear another series of intervals played harmonically and melodically. Use the tips to help you figure out which interval is being played. Again, remember to hum them, and also hum the notes in between the interval pitches to determine the correct interval. This time, the intervals utilize different tonics.

🔊 **TRACK 76**

1. _____	6. _____	11. _____
2. _____	7. _____	12. _____
3. _____	8. _____	13. _____
4. _____	9. _____	14. _____
5. _____	10. _____	

Again, interval recognition takes a lot of practice, so don't get frustrated. Just stick with it, as it opens up all kinds of musical doors.

Ear Training 10.4

This is a transcription exercise. The following are tracks with melodies that have melodic jumps. Previously, you transcribed melodies that only moved in stepwise patterns, but for these melodies, you have to use your broader knowledge of intervals. Listen to each track as many times as it takes to build and fine-tune your transcription. You could write the rhythm above the staff on your first listen and then start to figure out and write down the pitches on the staff. Go note by note, figuring out each interval and writing it down—don't try to do it all in one or two listens.

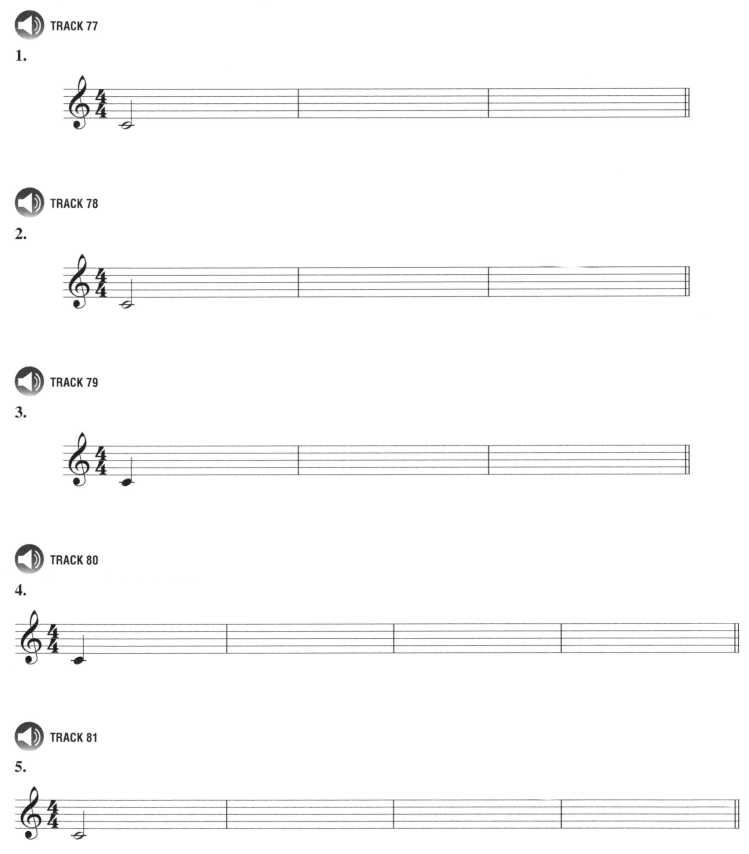

TRACK 77

1.

TRACK 78

2.

TRACK 79

3.

TRACK 80

4.

TRACK 81

5.

MOVEABLE INTERVAL SHAPES

The following are diagrams showing common and helpful interval shapes that can be played anywhere on the fretboard. They are broken down by string sets. Notice that the shapes for each interval are the same for every string set except where the tuning between the 3rd and 2nd strings affects them. In these cases, a simple half-step adjustment is all that is required.

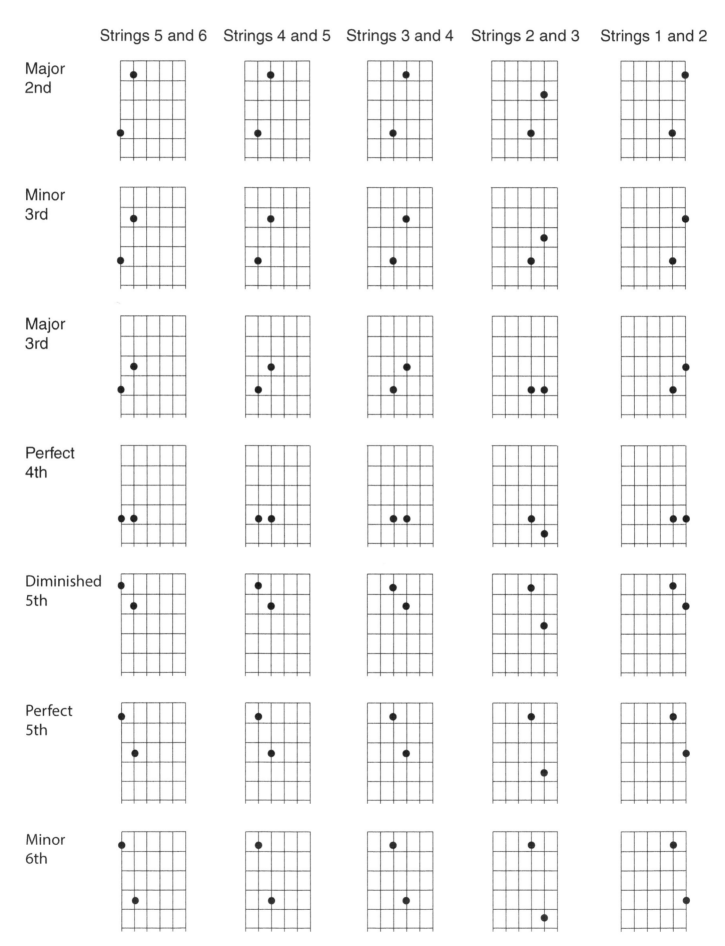

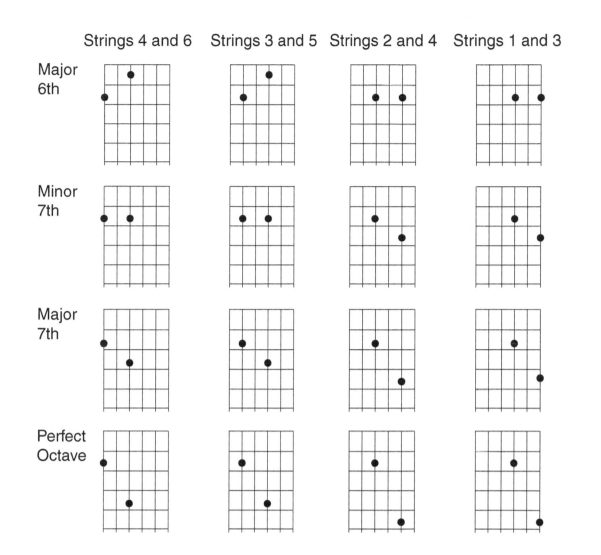

| | Strings 4 and 6 | Strings 3 and 5 | Strings 2 and 4 | Strings 1 and 3 |

Major 6th

Minor 7th

Major 7th

Perfect Octave

These shapes should all be memorized and played in as many locations on the fretboard as possible. Eventually, you will be able to hear an interval in a piece of music and automatically play it on the guitar.

Chapter 11: CHORDS

An interval is comprised of two notes, but a *chord* consists of three or more notes played at the same time. In this chapter, we'll look at several types of chords and how they are built from intervals.

A *triad* is a three-note chord made up of a *root* (upon which the chord is built and after which the chord is named), 3rd, and 5th. These notes are consecutive 3rds, or every *other* note in a scale, starting with the root. For example:

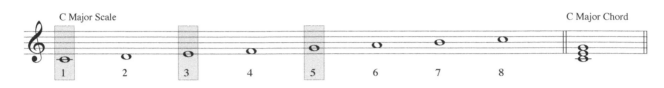

There are four different qualities of triads: *major*, *minor*, *augmented*, and *diminished*. We can look at the components of these chords in a couple of ways:

- **Intervals from the root:** e.g., root–3rd–5th (in other words, root–major 3rd–perfect 5th)
- **Intervals from note to note:** e.g., major 3rd–minor 3rd

We'll learn about the different types of triads by using both of the approaches mentioned above.

MAJOR TRIAD

A *major triad* is comprised of a root, major 3rd, and perfect 5th. From note to note, it contains two intervals: a major 3rd and a minor 3rd.

C Major (C): C (root)—E (3rd)—G (5th)

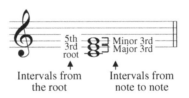

Note: *Chord symbols* are used to signify chords. As each new chord is introduced in this section, the chord symbol will appear to the right of the full chord name and in parentheses. For example, if you look above, the chord symbol "C" follows the full chord name, "C major" (major chords are simply known by their letter name).

Assignment 11.1

In the following examples, build major triads on the roots that are provided. When your root is a line note, your chord tones are on consecutive lines. When your root is a space note, your chord tones are on consecutive spaces. This process is called *stacking 3rds*, and you can think of it as building snowmen. You will have to apply accidentals to various notes to keep the major triad formula intact. The first example is done for you.

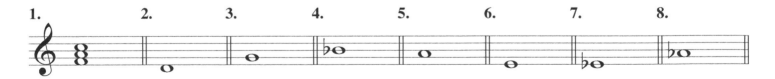

MINOR TRIAD

A *minor triad* is comprised of a root, minor 3rd (which can also be referred to as a ♭3rd), and perfect 5th. From note to note, it contains two intervals: a minor 3rd and a major 3rd.

C Minor (Cm): C (root)—E♭ (♭3rd)—G (5th)

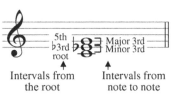

Intervals from the root | Intervals from note to note

Assignment 11.2

In the following examples, build minor triads on the roots that are provided.

AUGMENTED TRIAD

An *augmented triad* is comprised of a root, major 3rd, and augmented 5th (which can also be referred to as a ♯5th). From note to note, it contains two intervals: a major 3rd and a major 3rd.

C Augmented (C+): C (root)—E (3rd)—G♯ (♯5th)

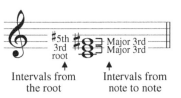

Intervals from the root | Intervals from note to note

Assignment 11.3

Build augmented triads on the roots provided.

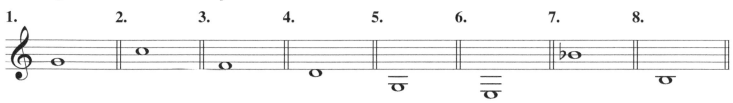

DIMINISHED TRIAD

A *diminished triad* is comprised of a root, minor 3rd, and diminished 5th (also known as a ♭5th). From note to note, it contains two intervals: a minor 3rd and a minor 3rd.

C Diminished (C°): C (root)—E♭ (♭3rd)—G♭ (♭5th)

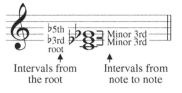

Intervals from the root | Intervals from note to note

Assignment 11.4

Build diminished triads on the roots provided.

GETTING TO KNOW THE SOUNDS OF CHORDS

Ear Training 11.1

Below, we have a major chord, minor chord, augmented chord, and diminished chord. All of them are played in open position and have the same root, D. By playing these one after the other, you will become acquainted with the differences between them. Try them:

 TRACK 82

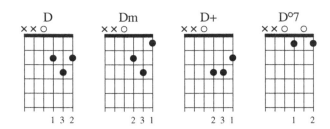

Note: Our diminished chord actually adds a fourth note, a diminished 7th, to the triad, resulting in D°7. We have included it here for the sake of playability.

Another note: Chord tones do not have to appear in the order that they are written on the staff for the chord to maintain its quality. Also, you can repeat any of the tones any number of times within the chord, but it remains a "triad."

Major vs. Minor

Play and listen to the D major chord and the D minor chord. Play them over and over, back and forth. There is only one note that changes: the F# in D major becomes an F natural in D minor. But it makes a big difference! Notice how the major chord has a brighter, more upbeat sound, while the minor chord has a darker, more introspective quality.

 TRACK 83

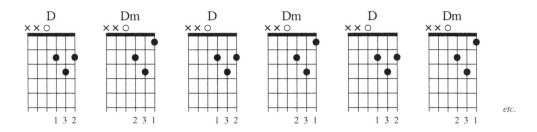

Major vs. Augmented

Now play and listen to the D major and D augmented chords. Again, play them over and over, back and forth. There is only one note that changes: the A in D major becomes an A# in D augmented. Notice how the major chord has a stable, even sound, while the augmented chord feels unsettled, like it needs to go somewhere else and cannot rest easy.

TRACK 84

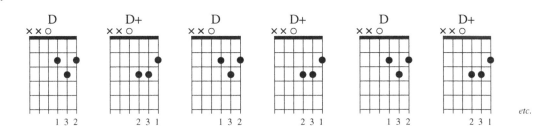

Minor vs. Diminished

Now play and listen to the D minor and D diminished chords. Again, play them over and over, back and forth. Though a bit melancholy, the minor chord sounds stable, or settled, while the diminished chord feels very unsettled. The latter is the sound used in old movies when the villain is tying someone to the train tracks.

 TRACK 85

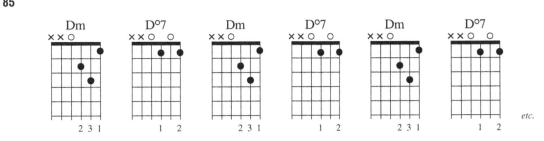

Quiz

On Track 86, you will hear a series of chords. In the blanks, write whether you think each chord is **major**, **minor**, **augmented**, or **diminished**.

 TRACK 86

1. _____

2. _____

3. _____

4. _____

5. _____

6. _____

7. _____

8. _____

9. _____

10. _____

11. _____

12. _____

Chapter 12: MAJOR DIATONIC HARMONY

Harmony is created when notes are sounded simultaneously to produce chords. The term *diatonic* means "belonging to the key." So, *major diatonic harmony* refers to all the chords that belong to a particular major key. We'll look at how this system works using triads.

To find the diatonic harmony belonging to any key, we need to stack 3rds on top of each scale tone. (Remember, to stack 3rds means to add every *other* note from the scale.) If we stack two 3rds on top of each scale tone, we have a series of triads. We'll start with the C major scale. Because there are seven scale tones, there are seven different chords in the key of C major.

🔊 **TRACK 87**

C Major Scale Harmonized

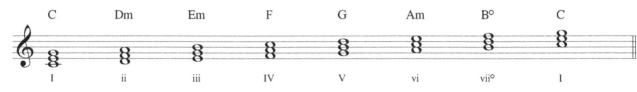

The order of chords in every major key is always the same:

Major—minor—minor—Major—Major—minor—diminished—Major

As can be seen above, Roman numerals indicate a chord's position in a given key. Uppercase Romans indicate major chords, lowercase Romans are used for minor chords, and lowercase Romans followed by a degree symbol (°) are used for diminished chords. So, if you were to mention the ii chord ("two chord") in the key of C, you would be talking about Dm. If you mentioned the vi chord ("six chord") in the key of C, you would be talking about Am. This makes it easy to talk about a *chord progression* (a series of chords) without limiting yourself to a specific key. We'll talk more about that in a bit. Suffice it to say, it is a musical shorthand—a way to describe a chord's function and place within a key that can apply to *all* keys.

> **Roman Numeral Review**
>
> | | | |
> |---|---|---|
> | I, i | = | 1 |
> | II, ii | = | 2 |
> | III, iii | = | 3 |
> | IV, iv | = | 4 |
> | V, v | = | 5 |
> | VI, vi | = | 6 |
> | VII, vii | = | 7 |

MORE EXAMPLES

Let's look at a couple of other examples. Below is the harmonized A major scale. Notice that the chord qualities and Roman numerals are exactly the same as in the key of C.

 TRACK 88

A Major Scale Harmonized

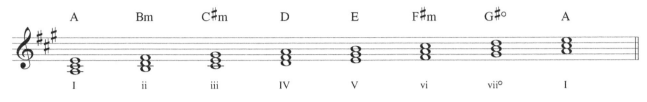

Here's one more example, this time in the key of E major.

 TRACK 89

E Major Scale Harmonized

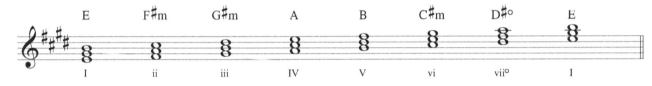

As you can see, the diatonic triads of a major key can be broken down as follows:

Major	I, IV, V
Minor	ii, iii, vi
Diminished	vii°

Assignment 12.1

Now it's your turn to figure out the chords in various keys, and you won't even have to write the notes to do it. All you need to know is how to play a major scale and be able to apply the order of chord qualities listed earlier: Major—minor—minor—Major—Major—minor—diminished—Major. If you can play any major scale on a single string, you can figure out the chord roots as well. For example, I know that the scale tones in Bb major are Bb–C–D–Eb–F–G–A–Bb, so our chords in the key of Bb are Bb–Cm–Dm–Eb–F–Gm–A°–Bb.

Write out the chords, in order, for the following keys. **Tip:** Write down the root notes first (consecutive letter names, then accidentals if required) and then fill in the chord qualities.

1. **F Major:** ____–____–____–____–____–____–____–____

2. **G Major:** ____–____–____–____–____–____–____–____

3. **Eb Major:** ____–____–____–____–____–____–____–____

4. **D Major:** ____–____–____–____–____–____–____–____

Answer the following questions:

5. What is the ii chord in the key of B♭? _____

6. What is the I chord in the key of G? _____

7. What is the vi chord in the key of C? _____

8. What is the IV chord in the key of A♭? _____

Use Roman numerals to answer the following:

9. What chord is Dm in the key of B♭? _____

10. What chord is F#° in the key of G? _____

11. What chord is F in the key of F? _____

12. What chord is A in the key of D? _____

Let's play through one of these harmonized scales. Remember: the notes within each chord do not have to be in any particular order, just present—plus, they can even be doubled or tripled. This brings us to the term *voicing*. There are many possible voicings for any given chord. Even though a chord is played differently, the qualities and letter names of these chords remain the same. For example, the following are several different voicings for a C major chord:

C Major Chords

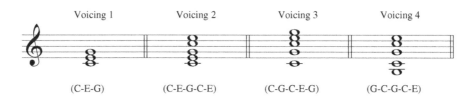

Voicing 1   Voicing 2   Voicing 3   Voicing 4

(C-E-G)   (C-E-G-C-E)   (C-G-C-E-G)   (G-C-G-C-E)

Let's use first-position voicings to play a harmonized scale in the key of C major. (**Note:** Our vii chord, B°7, has an additional chord tone, the diminished 7th, for ease of playing and a more aesthetically pleasing sound than the regular diminished triad. Additionally, it is technically a second-position chord.) Play through the following:

🔊 **TRACK 90**

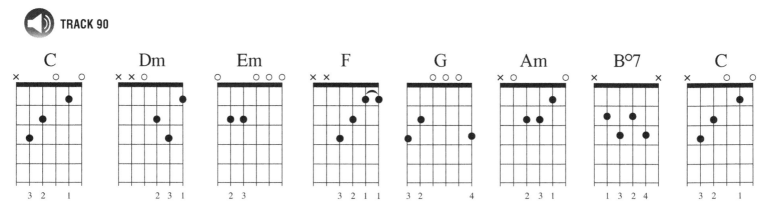

You can try playing through the diatonic chords in any key. (If you know some moveable barre chords, this can be very easy to do.)

PRIMARY CHORDS

The three major chords in a key—I, IV, and V—are known as the *primary chords*, or *principle chords*. Many different chord progressions use these chords. It's easy to find the primary chords in any key: just figure out the scale tones and then play major chords on top of those notes. For example, let's look at the key of G:

1. We know that G is the I chord because that is our key.

2. Count up four from G, G–A–B–C, and we find that C is our IV chord.

3. Count up one more from the IV chord, C–D, and we see that D is our V chord.

4. Our primary chords in the key of G major are: G, C, and D.

Assignment 12.2

1. What are the primary chords in the key of F? _____

2. What are the primary chords in the key of D? _____

3. What are the primary chords in the key of A? _____

4. What are the primary chords in the key of E? _____

CHORD PROGRESSIONS

Songs are made from chord progressions. A chord progression is a series of chords that repeats throughout a piece of music. We can describe these chord progressions by using the Roman numerals of diatonic harmony. Remember, by using Roman numerals, we are identifying a progression that can be played in *any* key. To get specific, we would have to mention the key name; for instance, a I–IV–V progression in the key of B♭ would indicate the use of the chords B♭, E♭, and F. Let's look at some very common chord progressions used in guitar music.

I–V Progression

The I–V progression features two of the primary chords and is very common. In the key of C major, our I and V chords are C and G. (**Note:** The examples in this section use *slash notation*, which is just an unspecified rhythm or strum pattern. You can use any pattern you'd like to try these chords.)

 TRACK 91

I–V Progression in C Major

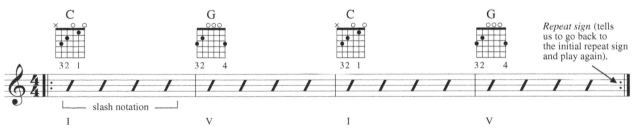

Here's one more, this time in the key of D. Here, the I chord is D and the V chord is A.

TRACK 92

I–V Progression in D Major

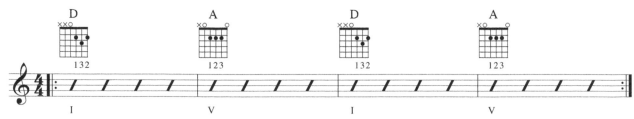

You can see that the pattern is one measure of the I chord, one measure of the V chord, and back and forth. Let's look at some more progressions.

I–IV–V–IV Progression

The I–IV–V–IV progression features all three of the primary chords and is used in songs like "La Bamba" and "What I Like About You." In the key of C major, the I, IV, and V chords are C, F, and G.

TRACK 93

I–IV–V–IV Progression in C Major

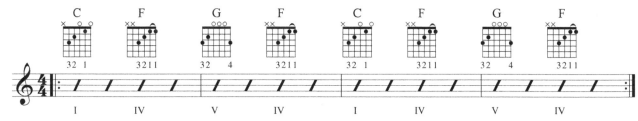

Let's play the above progression in the key of G. The I chord will be G, the IV chord will be C, and the V chord will be D.

TRACK 94

I–IV–V–IV Progression in G Major

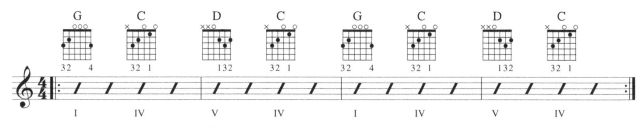

Again, notice how, even though the chords are being replaced, the Roman numerals and the sound of the progression remain the same.

I–vi–IV–V Progression

This progression adds a minor chord to the mix: the vi chord. In the key of C major, our vi chord is Am. Many songs have featured this chord progression, one of the most well-known being "Unchained Melody," made famous by the Righteous Brothers.

 TRACK 95

I–vi–IV–V Progression in C Major

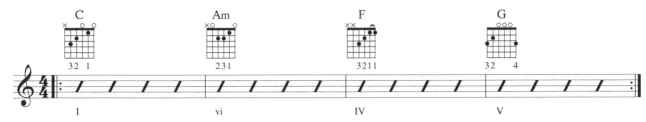

Now plug into this progression the chords from the key of G major: G (I), Em (vi), C (IV), and D (V).

 TRACK 96

I–vi–IV–V Progression in G Major

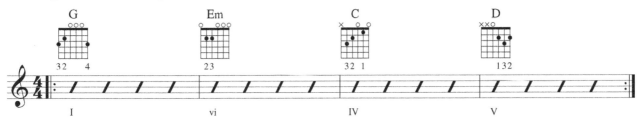

The Blues Progression

What would guitar music be without the blues progression? This is one of the most common progressions around. Though there are many variations, we will just show a simple 12-measure version. To play a basic 12-bar blues progression, we will need just our I, IV, and IV chords. Let's check it out first in the key of C:

 TRACK 97

Blues Progression in C Major

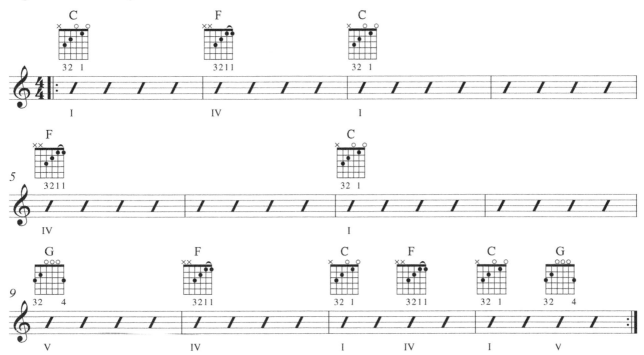

Now let's plug in the primary chords from the key of A: A (I), D (IV), and E (V).

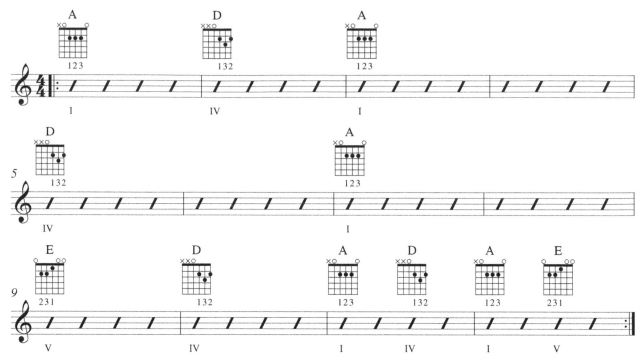 TRACK 98

Blues Progression in A Major

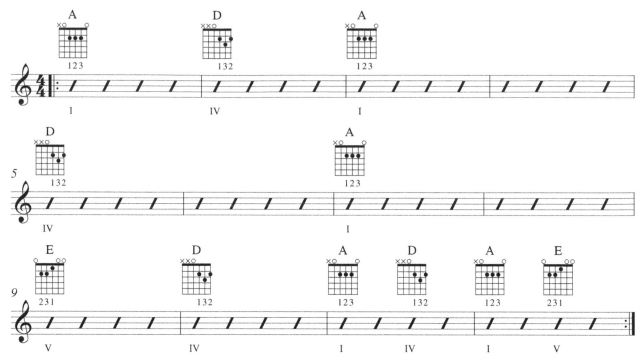

The process of moving a piece of music to a different key is called *transposition*. When you transpose a song or chord progression, you are keeping the relationships between all of the notes and chords the same, just moving everything to a different pitch range.

Assignment 12.3

Below is a series of chord progressions shown in Roman numerals. Transpose each one to the keys specified under the staffs. Write the chord symbols (G, Dm, Em, etc.) in the blanks provided.

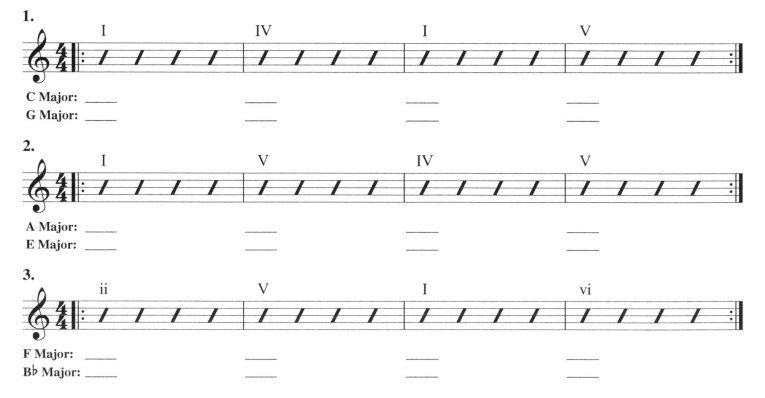

82

Analyze the chord progressions below. The chords and keys will be given—you just have to fill in the blanks with the correct Roman numerals.

4.

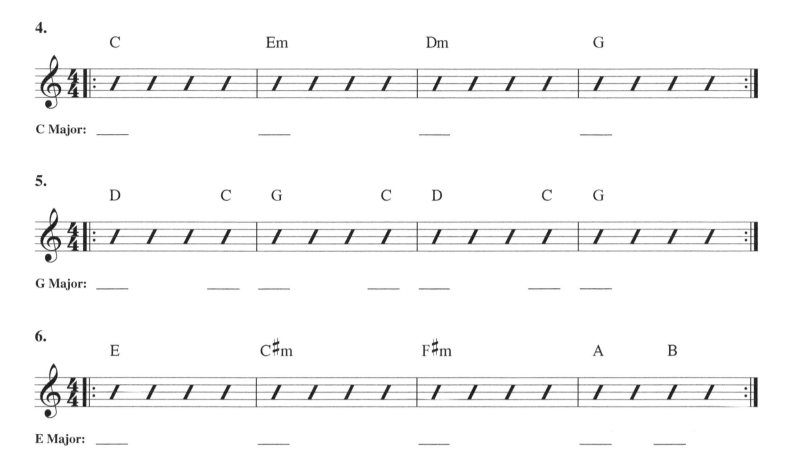

C Major: _____   _____   _____   _____

5.

G Major: _____   _____   _____   _____   _____   _____   _____

6.

E Major: _____   _____   _____   _____   _____

Ear Training 12.1

Listen to the following tracks and write the correct Roman numerals for the chord progressions in the blanks. Start by trying to identify and hum the root notes of the chords. If you can find the scale degree that the chord is built on, you can then apply the correct quality, depending on where the chord falls within the key.

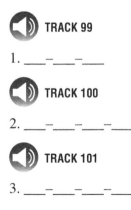 **TRACK 99**

1. ____ – ____ – ____

TRACK 100

2. ____ – ____ – ____ – ____

TRACK 101

3. ____ – ____ – ____ – ____

Chapter 13: THE MINOR SCALE

RELATIVE MINOR

Every major scale has a *relative minor*, which is built on the 6th degree of the former. What this means is that the relative major and minor share the same key signature; the same notes are used, as well, just starting and ending in a different place. So, if we were to look at the C major scale and start with the 6th scale degree, A, and end with A, we would have the A minor scale, which is the relative minor of C major.

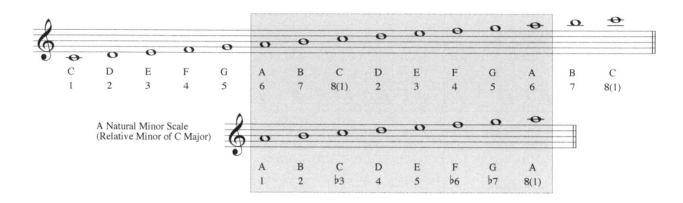

There are three types of minor scales: *natural minor*, *harmonic minor*, and *melodic minor*. Let's look at all three.

NATURAL MINOR

As seen above, when you start and end with the 6th scale degree of any major scale, the result is a natural minor scale. The formula in scale degrees is: 1–2–♭3–4–5–♭6–♭7–8. (**Note:** Any time a scale degree is lowered or raised in relation to the degrees of a major scale, a flat or sharp appears before it.) The natural minor scale has its own step formula, as well: whole–half–whole–whole–half–whole–whole. (**Note:** We have included one open-position fingering with each of these scales, but feel free to try them on a single string or in moveable forms of your own.)

 TRACK 102

A Natural Minor Scale

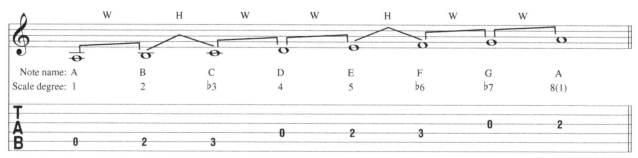

HARMONIC MINOR

The harmonic minor scale has a more exotic sound and is often used to harmonize music in minor keys. To create a harmonic minor scale, start with a natural minor scale and raise the 7th degree, which becomes a natural 7th. The formula in scale degrees is: 1–2–♭3–4–5–♭6–7. The step formula for the harmonic minor scale is: whole–half–whole–whole–half–whole+half–half.

 TRACK 103

A Harmonic Minor Scale

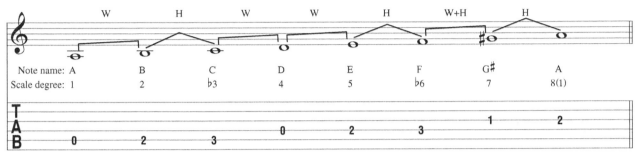

MELODIC MINOR

The melodic minor scale is often used to create melodies. It is unique in that it is different when ascending and descending. The ascending form is like the natural minor scale but with a natural 6th and natural 7th (this can also be thought of as being like the major scale but with a ♭3rd). The descending form is exactly like the natural minor scale. So, the scale degrees for the ascending form are: 1–2–♭3–4–5–6–7. The step formula for the ascending form is: whole–half–whole–whole–whole–whole–half.

 TRACK 104

A Melodic Minor Scale

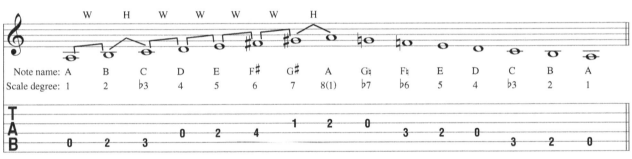

Assignment 13.1

In the blank spaces provided, write the relative minor scales of the indicated major scales.

Major Scales	Relative Minor
1. G Major	_____
2. D Major	_____
3. F Major	_____
4. E♭ Major	_____
5. A Major	_____
6. E Major	_____
7. A♭ Major	_____
8. F♯ Major	_____

Below, notate the E natural minor scale. Then turn it into the E harmonic minor scale and, finally, the E melodic minor scale (ascending form). In addition to the standard notation, include note names and scale degrees.

9. E Natural Minor Scale

Note
name: ____   ____   ____   ____   ____   ____   ____   ____

Scale
degree: ____   ____   ____   ____   ____   ____   ____   ____

10. E Harmonic Minor Scale

Note
name: ____   ____   ____   ____   ____   ____   ____   ____

Scale
degree: ____   ____   ____   ____   ____   ____   ____   ____

11. E Melodic Minor Scale (Ascending Form)

Note
name: ____   ____   ____   ____   ____   ____   ____   ____

Scale
degree: ____   ____   ____   ____   ____   ____   ____   ____

As a bonus, see if you can notate the *E minor pentatonic scale*, a five-note scale that consists of scale degrees 1–♭3–4–5–♭7. (**Note:** We include the octave of the tonic, so there are six notes to fill in.)

12. E Minor Pentatonic Scale

Note
name: ____   ____   ____   ____   ____   ____

Scale
degree: ____   ____   ____   ____   ____   ____

On Track 105, you will hear a series of scales. Write in the blanks below if you think the scale is **natural minor**, **harmonic minor**, **melodic minor**, or **minor pentatonic**. Listen for the notes that are altered when creating these scales—namely, scale degrees 6 and 7.

TRACK 105

1. _____   5. _____

2. _____   6. _____

3. _____   7. _____

4. _____   8. _____

A NOTE ABOUT MINOR KEYS

Keys also come from minor scales. A *minor key* usually indicates the presence of the harmonic or melodic minor scales. The reason for this is that traditional theory necessitates the presence of a *leading tone* (the natural/major 7th) to have a true "key." When the natural minor scale is used to create melodies, it is considered a mode (the natural minor scale being the sixth *mode*—the *Aeolian* mode—of the major scale).

So, when referencing a relative minor "key," you will most likely be referring to a tonal structure using either the harmonic minor or melodic minor scale.

CONCLUSION

Congratulations on coming to the end of our *Guitar Theory Workbook*. We have covered a ton of useful, but sometimes challenging, concepts. Hopefully, it is all clear to you, but if not, don't worry about it—this stuff takes time. As long as you keep trying to learn theory and applying it to your playing, you will eventually understand it all. The musical trip is marked by many "a-ha, I finally get it!" moments. Often, the ideas seem so simple once you grasp them. Each revelation shines a light on more advanced concepts, and in this way, you continue to ascend the ladder of musical understanding. Our most important advice is to keep studying theory and *use* what you learn. You'll see that it's more than worth the effort!

ANSWER KEY

Chapter 1

Assignment 1.1

I Rosette

E Neck

H Soundhole

A Headstock

O Position Markers

C Tuning Pegs

M Bridge Pins

B Capstan (String Post)

D Nut

P Frets

L Saddle

G Body

K Bridge

J Pick Guard

N Strings

F Fretboard (Fingerboard)

Assignment 1.2

J Whammy Bar

E Neck

O Output Jack

D Headstock

F Position Markers

B Tuning Pegs

I Pickups

C Capstan (String Post)

N Volume and Tone Controls

M Pickup Selector

A Nut

H Frets

R Saddles

P Body

Q Bridge

K Pick Guard

L Strings

G Fretboard (Fingerboard)

Assignment 1.3

1. 6th string, 1st fret

   5th string, 3rd fret

   4th string, 5th fret

   1st string, 1st fret

2. 5th string, 7th fret

   4th string, 6th fret

   3rd string, 8th fret

   2nd string, 7th fret

3. 3rd string, 10th fret

   3rd string, 12th fret

   2nd string, 10th fret

   2nd string, 13th fret

   1st string, 10th fret

   1st string, 13th fret

4. 6th string, 1st fret

   5th string, 4th fret

   4th string, 3rd fret

   3rd string, 1st fret

   2nd string, 1st fret

   2nd string, 2nd fret

   1st string, 4th fret

Assignment 1.4

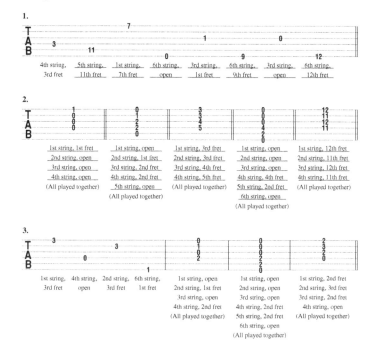

Chapter 2

Assignment 2.1

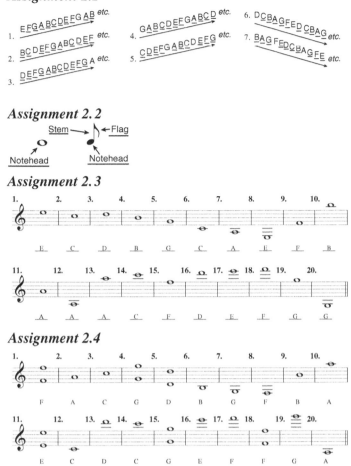

Assignment 2.2

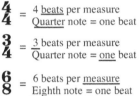

Assignment 2.3

(measures 1–10)
E C D B G C A E F B

(measures 11–20)
A A A C F D E F G G

Assignment 2.4

(measures 1–10)
F A C G D B G F B A

(measures 11–20)
E C D C G E F F G A

Assignment 2.5

a) <u>Ex.1</u>   e) <u>Ex. 3</u>

b) <u>Ex. 10</u>   f) <u>Ex. 19</u>

c) <u>Ex. 13</u>   g) <u>Ex. 15</u>

d) <u>Ex. 18</u>   h) <u>Ex. 4</u>

i) <u>Ex. 5</u>   m) <u>Ex. 17</u>

j) <u>Ex. 7</u>   n) <u>Ex. 7</u>

k) <u>Ex. 4</u>   o) <u>Ex. 16</u>

l) <u>Ex. 11</u>   p) <u>Ex. 8</u>

Ear Training 2.1

🔊 TRACK 2   🔊 TRACK 3

1. Note 1   10. Note 1

2. Note 2   11. Note 2

3. Note 2   12. Note 1

4. Note 1   13. Note 1

5. Note 2   14. Note 2

6. Note 1   15. Note 2

7. Note 2   16. Same

8. Same   17. Note 1

9. Note 2   18. Note 2

Chapter 3

Assignment 3.1

A. <u>measure</u>

B. <u>bar line</u>

C. <u>measure</u>

D. <u>measure</u>

E. <u>bar line</u>

F. <u>double bar line</u>

G. <u>measure</u>

H. <u>terminal bar line</u>

Assignment 3.2

4/4 = 4 <u>beats</u> per measure
<u>Quarter</u> note = one beat

3/4 = <u>3</u> beats per measure
<u>Quarter</u> note = <u>one</u> beat

6/8 = 6 beats per <u>measure</u>
<u>Eighth</u> note = one beat

3/8 = <u>3</u> beats per measure
<u>Eighth</u> note = <u>one</u> beat

Assignment 3.3

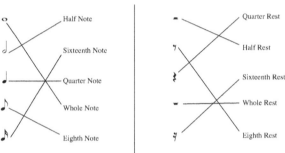

Assignment 3.4

1. <u>Four</u>

2. <u>One</u>

3. <u>Four</u>

4. <u>Four</u>

5. <u>Neither; they last for the same amount of time</u>

6. <u>Two</u>

7. <u>Sixteen</u>

Assignment 3.5

Ear Training 3.1

TRACK 8

Ex. 1

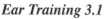

TRACK 9

Ex. 2

TRACK 10

Ex. 3

TRACK 11

Ex. 4

Assignment 3.6

1. 2-1/2
2. 3/4
3. 5

4. 3/4
5. 3/4
6. 3/8 (sixteenth note = 1/4 beat, half of 1/4 is 1/8.   1/4 + 1/8 = 2/8 + 1/8 = 3/8) That was a tricky one!

Assignment 3.7

Ex. 1

Ex. 2

Ex. 3

Ex. 4

Ex. 5

Ex. 6

Ear Training 3.2

TRACK 12

(**Note:** Technically, for the first measure, you could tie a half note to a quarter note. However, the intention with notation is always clarity and simplicity, so the dotted half note is preferable.)

Ex. 1

TRACK 13

Ex. 2

TRACK 14

Ex. 3

TRACK 15

Ex. 4

Chapter 4

Assignment 4.1

The answers are in gray.

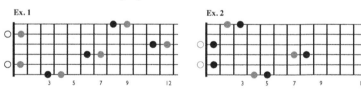

Ear Training 4.1

TRACK 17

1. lower
2. lower

3. higher
4. lower

5. higher
6. higher

7. higher
8. lower

9. lower
10. higher

Assignment 4.2

The answers are in gray.

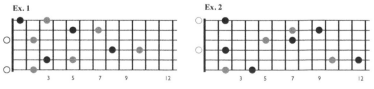

Ear Training 4.2

TRACK 19

1. <u>higher</u> 3. <u>lower</u> 5. <u>lower</u> 7. <u>lower</u> 9. <u>lower</u>

2. <u>higher</u> 4. <u>lower</u> 6. <u>lower</u> 8. <u>higher</u> 10. <u>higher</u>

Assignment 4.3

1. <u>H</u>   3. <u>W</u>   5. <u>H</u>

2. <u>H</u>   4. <u>W</u>   6. <u>W</u>

Ear Training 4.3

TRACK 21

1. <u>H</u>   5. <u>H</u>   9. <u>H</u>   13. <u>H</u>

2. <u>W</u>   6. <u>W</u>   10. <u>W</u>   14. <u>W</u>

3. <u>W</u>   7. <u>H</u>   11. <u>W</u>   15. <u>H</u>

4. <u>H</u>   8. <u>W</u>   12. <u>W</u>   16. <u>H</u>

Chapter 5

Ear Training 5.1

TRACK 23

Ex. 1

TRACK 24

Ex. 2

TRACK 25

Ex. 3

TRACK 26

Ex. 4

TRACK 27

Ex. 5

Chapter 6

Assignment 6.1

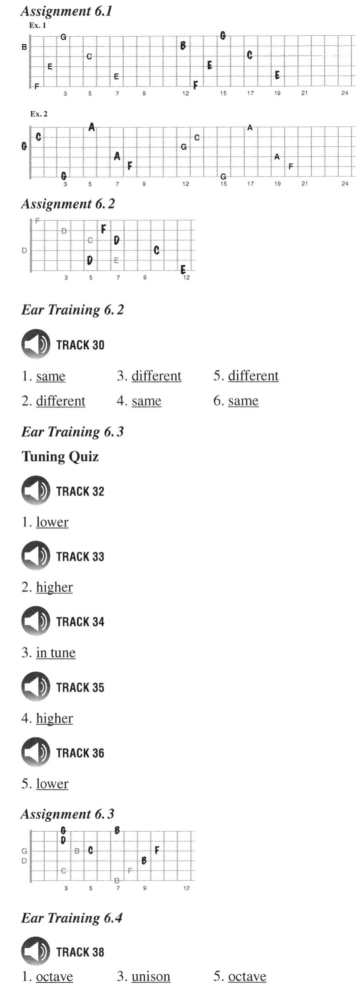

Ex. 1

Ex. 2

Assignment 6.2

Ear Training 6.2

TRACK 30

1. <u>same</u>   3. <u>different</u>   5. <u>different</u>

2. <u>different</u>   4. <u>same</u>   6. <u>same</u>

Ear Training 6.3

Tuning Quiz

TRACK 32

1. <u>lower</u>

TRACK 33

2. <u>higher</u>

TRACK 34

3. <u>in tune</u>

TRACK 35

4. <u>higher</u>

TRACK 36

5. <u>lower</u>

Assignment 6.3

Ear Training 6.4

TRACK 38

1. <u>octave</u>   3. <u>unison</u>   5. <u>octave</u>

2. <u>unison</u>   4. <u>octave</u>   6. <u>unison</u>

Chapter 7

Assignment 7.1

Assignment 7.2

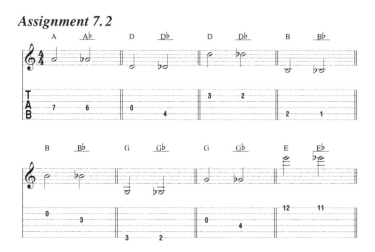

Assignment 7.3

Assignment 7.4

Assignment 7.5

Assignment 7.6

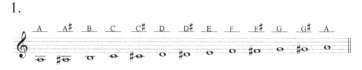

Assignment 7.7

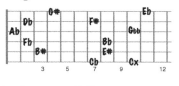

Assignment 7.8

1.

2.

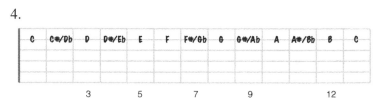

3.

4.

5a.

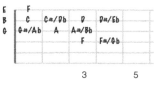

5b.

Chapter 8

Assignment 8.1

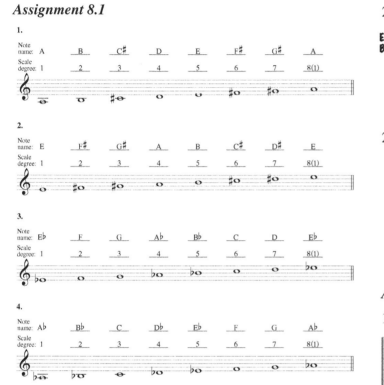

Assignment 8.2

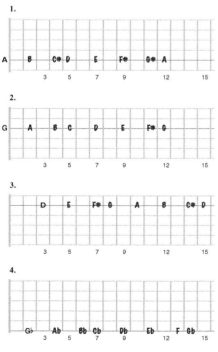

1a.

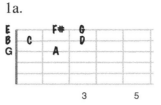

1b.

2a.

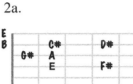

2b.

Assignment 8.4

1.

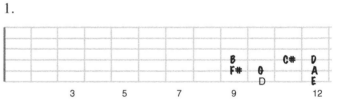

2.

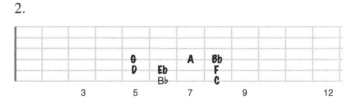

Ear Training 8.1

 **TRACK 56**

1. NO   7

 **TRACK 57**

2. NO   3

 **TRACK 58**

3. NO   4

TRACK 59

4. YES

TRACK 60

5. YES

TRACK 61

6. NO   2

TRACK 62

7. YES

TRACK 63

8. YES

Chapter 9

Assignment 9.1

Assignment 9.2

1. D Major	6. Db Major	11. C# Major
2. Eb Major	7. F# Major	12. Ab Major
3. Cb Major	8. F Major	13. Gb Major
4. A Major	9. Bb Major	14. C Major
5. E Major	10. G Major	15. B Major

Assignment 9.3

1. G#
2. Eb
3. A
4. Eb
5.

6.

7.

8.

9. B
10. Db
11. F#
12. Gb

Chapter 10

Ear Training 10.1

TRACK 68

1. Major 3rd	5. Perfect octave
2. Perfect 5th	6. Major 2nd
3. Major 6th	7. Major 7th
4. Perfect unison	8. Perfect 4th

TRACK 69

9. Major 3rd	13. Perfect octave
10. Perfect 5th	14. Major 2nd
11. Major 6th	15. Major 7th
12. Perfect unison	16. Perfect 4th

Assignment 10.1

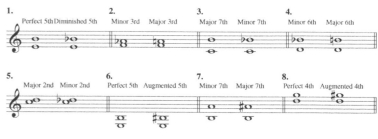

Ear Training 10.2

TRACK 73

1. major <u>2nd</u> minor <u>1st</u>

2. major <u>1st</u> minor <u>2nd</u>

3. minor <u>2nd</u> major <u>1st</u>

4. major <u>2nd</u> minor <u>1st</u>

5. diminished <u>2nd</u> minor <u>1st</u>

6. perfect <u>1st</u> augmented <u>2nd</u>

7. augmented <u>2nd</u> perfect <u>1st</u>

8. major <u>1st</u> minor <u>2nd</u>

Ear Training 10.3

TRACK 75

1. <u>minor 3rd</u>

2. <u>major 2nd</u>

3. <u>perfect 5th</u>

4. <u>augmented 5th/minor 6th</u>

5. <u>major 7th</u>

6. <u>minor 7th</u>

7. <u>perfect octave</u>

8. <u>major 6th</u>

9. <u>perfect unison</u>

10. <u>augmented 4th/diminished 5th</u>

11. <u>minor 2nd</u>

12. <u>perfect 4th</u>

13. <u>augmented 5th/minor 6th</u>

14. <u>major 3rd</u>

TRACK 76

1. major 3rd

2. augmented 4th/diminished 5th

3. perfect 4th

4. minor 2nd

5. augmented 4th/diminished 5th

6. perfect unison

7. major 6th

8. perfect octave

9. minor 7th

10. major 7th

11. augmented 5th/minor 6th

12. perfect 5th

13. major 2nd

14. minor 3rd

Ear Training 10.4

TRACK 77

1.

TRACK 78

2.

TRACK 79

Note: For the B♭ in measure 2, A♯ is also acceptable.

TRACK 80

TRACK 81

Note: The F♯s in measures 2 and 3 are preferable, but G♭ is also acceptable.

Chapter 11

Assignment 11.1

Assignment 11.2

Assignment 11.3

Assignment 11.4

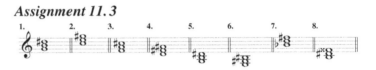

Ear Training 11.1

Quiz

TRACK 86

1. <u>major</u>

2. <u>major</u>

3. <u>minor</u>

4. <u>augmented</u>

5. <u>diminished</u>

6. <u>major</u>

7. <u>minor</u>

8. <u>minor</u>

9. <u>major</u>

10. <u>augmented</u>

11. <u>minor</u>

12. <u>diminished</u>

Chapter 12

Assignment 12.1

1. **F Major:** <u>F</u>–<u>Gm</u>–<u>Am</u>–<u>Bb</u>–<u>C</u>–<u>Dm</u>–<u>E°</u>–<u>F</u>

2. **G Major:** <u>G</u>–<u>Am</u>–<u>Bm</u>–<u>C</u>–<u>D</u>–<u>Em</u>–<u>F#°</u>–<u>G</u>

3. **Eb Major:** <u>Eb</u>–<u>Fm</u>–<u>Gm</u>–<u>Ab</u>–<u>Bb</u>–<u>Cm</u>–<u>D°</u>–<u>Eb</u>

4. **D Major:** <u>D</u>–<u>Em</u>–<u>F#m</u>–<u>G</u>–<u>A</u>–<u>Bm</u>–<u>C#°</u>–<u>D</u>

5. <u>Cm</u>

6. <u>G</u>

7. <u>Am</u>

8. <u>Db</u>

9. <u>iii</u>

10. <u>vii°</u>

11. <u>I</u>

12. <u>V</u>

Assignment 12.2

1. <u>F, Bb, C</u>

2. <u>D, G, A</u>

3. <u>A, D, E</u>

4. <u>E, A, B</u>

Assignment 12.3

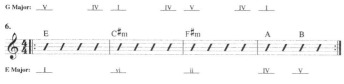

Ear Training 12.1

TRACK 99

1. <u>I</u>–<u>IV</u>–<u>V</u>

TRACK 100

2. <u>I</u>–<u>V</u>–<u>vi</u>–<u>IV</u>

TRACK 101

3. <u>I</u>–<u>vi</u>–<u>ii</u>–<u>V</u>

Chapter 13

Assignment 13.1

1. <u>E Minor</u>

2. <u>B Minor</u>

3. <u>D Minor</u>

4. <u>C Minor</u>

5. <u>F# Minor</u>

6. <u>C# Minor</u>

7. <u>F Minor</u>

8. <u>D# Minor</u>

9. **E Natural Minor Scale**

10. **E Harmonic Minor Scale**

11. **E Melodic Minor Scale**

12. **E Minor Pentatonic Scale**

Ear Training 13.1

TRACK 105

1. <u>natural minor</u>   5. <u>harmonic minor</u>

2. <u>melodic minor</u>   6. <u>natural minor</u>

3. <u>harmonic minor</u>   7. <u>melodic minor</u>

4. <u>minor pentatonic</u>   8. <u>minor pentatonic</u>